KINGDOM

SPORTS

COLOSSIANS

THE COMPLETE ATHLETE

A BIBLE STUDY FOR ATHLETES
WHO WANT TO UNDERSTAND
HOW GOD DEVELOPS AND SPIRITUALLY MATURES

A 12-WEEK STUDY

JOSHUA THIESSEN

Colossians - The Complete Athlete

Cross Training Publishing

www.crosstrainingpublishing.com

(308) 293-3891

Copyright © 2024 by Joshua Thiessen

ISBN: 978-1-929478-81-1

FOREWORD

In an athlete's journey, the pursuit of excellence is often accompanied by challenges, triumphs, and moments of self-discovery. The Book of Colossians offers timeless wisdom that speaks directly to the heart of every competitor, reminding us that our identity and purpose extend far beyond the playing field. Authored by the Apostle Paul, this Epistle invites athletes to reflect on their true worth and the values that should guide their actions, both in sports and in life.

Athletes often face pressure to perform, but this letter reminds us that our worth is not solely defined by our achievements. Instead, it encourages us to cultivate a strong sense of character, resilience, and sportsmanship, allowing us to shine both in victory and defeat. By embodying these principles, you can inspire not only yourselves but also your teammates and competitors.

Ron Brown
Nebraska Football Assistant Coach
Co-founder of Kingdom Sports

TABLE OF CONTENTS

THE COMPLETE ATHLETE . . .

GRATITUDE

I am profoundly grateful to the Lord for the opportunity to study His Word, which continually points towards spiritual maturity in Christ. I'm also deeply thankful to everyone who played a role in editing, proofing, and laying out this study—their dedication is vital. My prayer is that this study will encourage the reader to grow in the wisdom and understanding which is only found in the Christ, and that God will use it to in your life so that you may be presented "fully mature in Christ" (Colossians 1:28).

INTRODUCTION

As a Christian athlete, you are entrusted with more than just developing your athletic skills—you are called to shape character and cultivate maturity in your Christian walk. The book of Colossians provides us with a profound blueprint for this task, as it reveals how the fullness of life is found in Christ. Paul's letter encourages us to help others grow into spiritual maturity, being "complete in Christ" (Colossians 2:10), where their identity, purpose, and strength are firmly rooted. This study will guide you through the essential truths of Colossians, equipping you to foster deeper maturity and Christlikeness in your life and the lives of those you around you, preparing yourself for challenges both in sports and in life.

Understanding Colossians

Understanding the context of Colossians is essential for grasping its message of spiritual maturity. Written by the Apostle Paul around AD 60-62 while he was imprisoned in Rome, Colossians addresses the believers in the small but growing church in Colossae, a city in Asia Minor (modern-day Turkey). Paul had not visited the church personally but wrote in response to reports from Epaphras, a fellow servant of Christ, who shared concerns about false teachings threatening the church. These teachings, often a mix of Jewish legalism, pagan mysticism, and early forms of Gnosticism, undermined the sufficiency of Christ. Paul's purpose in writing was to affirm Christ's preeminence and to remind the Colossians that true maturity and completeness can only be found in Him. This message remains essential for today as you seek to mature in Christ, resisting anything that would distract from His all-sufficient work.

Relevance to Athletes

1. **Christ-Centered Life:**
   - Athletes are called to live with Christ at the center of their lives. This means modeling Christlike character, humility, and service, ensuring that our influence points others toward Him.

2. **Growth over Scoreboard:**
   - Paul encourages believers to be "rooted and built up in Christ." This principle reminds us that the role of athlete goes beyond developing physical or technical abilities or wins or loses. True success comes from how we conduct ourselves in God's economy.

3. **Pursuit of Excellence**
   - "Whatever you do, whether in word or deed, do it all in the name of the Lord Jesus." As athletes, pursuing excellence in both actions and words is not only essential, it is a theological imperative. The standard of true integrity is comprehensive in every area of life, both on and off the field.

4. **Build Strong, Christlike Relationships:**
   - Paul calls believers to "put on" virtues like compassion, kindness, humility, and patience and "put off" the old man's wrath, anger, malice, slander, and abusive speech. For athletes, helping foster a team environment marked by these virtues is vital. By emphasizing what should be put off as well what attributes should be put on, the athlete sets himself to grow in Christ.

Key Themes to Explore

- **The Supremacy and Sufficiency of Christ:** Colossians emphasizes that Christ is supreme over all creation and fully sufficient for salvation and sanctification. Paul declares Christ as the image of the invisible God and the one in whom all things were created (Colossians 1:15-20). This theme underscores that believers need nothing beyond Christ for spiritual growth, rejecting false teachings that undermine His preeminence.

- **Spiritual Maturity in Christ:** A major theme in Colossians is growing into spiritual maturity. Paul encourages believers to be "rooted and built up in Him" (Colossians 2:7) and calls them to "put on" Christlike virtues (Colossians 3:12-14). This theme highlights the process of becoming complete in Christ, emphasizing spiritual growth and transformation in everyday life.

- **Putting off the Old, Putting on the New:** Another key theme in Colossians is the ongoing process of sanctification, where believers are called to "put off" the old self and "put on" the new self in Christ (Colossians 3:9-10). This transformation involves leaving behind sinful behaviors and attitudes—anger, malice, slander, and immorality—and replacing them with Christlike virtues such as compassion, kindness, humility, and love (Colossians 3:12-14). Sanctification is not a one-time event but an ongoing process as believers grow in spiritual maturity, aligning their character with Christ. Paul emphasizes that this change is empowered by the believer's new identity in Christ, and it affects every area of life, from personal relationships to public witness.

Conclusion

As you embark on this study of Colossians, approach each session with an open heart and mind, ready to uncover timeless truths that will deepen your spiritual maturity and strengthen your leadership both on and off the field. Colossians calls us to live lives that reflect the supremacy and sufficiency of Christ, challenging us to grow in wisdom, humility, and love. Through this study, may you come to better understand the sanctification process of putting off the old self and putting on the new self in Christ. I pray this study helps equip you and others toward spiritual maturity, grounded in a deeper relationship with Christ, and empowered to live for His glory in all you do.

Soli Deo Gloria,

Josh Thiessen

FORMAT

The format for this book is simple.
These are the parts of each chapter:

CHAPTER TITLE

Summarizes the key concept in one word or phrase.

STUDY STARTER

Helps you understand the importance and relevance of the spiritual truths you're about to study.

STUDY PASSAGE

Gives you the designated biblical text to read and study for the chapter.

STUDY HELP

Provides insight into the structure of the passage, meaning of words, interpretation of statements, and explanation of concepts.

STUDY QUESTIONS

Asks questions about the passage you must investigate and answer.

STUDY SUMMARY

Condenses the passage into one singular statement so you can understand the "big idea" of the text.

ATHLETE CONNECTION

Takes the Study Summary and transfers it to the world of sports so you can clearly see the Spirit-intended applications of the Word of God in the life as a Christian athlete.

KEYS TO WINNING

Guides you to meditate on the spiritual truths in the text and how they should shape your own heart and life as an athlete.

GAME CHANGER

Points you to the person and work of Jesus Christ to help you be a complete athlete through the power of the Gospel.

ONE BIG THING

Asks you to consider the most significant lesson you should take with you from the chapter.

IMPACT PRAYER

Motivates you to seek the Lord's help in applying the truths you have learned in each study.

STRATEGY

The strategy for this manual is also simple.
This is my recommendation:

Recruit a group of athletes to walk through the study with you. These athletes do not have to be Christians to join the study. As a matter of fact, I encourage you to reach out to any athlete you think would consider participating.

Secure a copy of this training manual for everyone who participates in the study. You can order more copies at www.crosstrainingpublishing.com

Appoint a leader for the weekly group study. This leader can be an athlete, a coach, former coach, spiritual leader, or pastor. The key criteria are that this person is a Christian who understands athletes, pursues Christ, and is willing to put in a little extra work to make the group study a powerful time in the Word of God. The group leader has the liberty to elaborate on the text and press into areas that are not necessarily covered in each lesson. This manual is merely a guide. There is freedom to take the study deeper and wider for more growth.

Schedule a weekly meeting day and time for 10-12 weeks. Allocate 45 to 60 minutes for the group study. Put the dates and times in your calendar and consider them a high priority.

Invest 30-60 minutes on your own prior to the study familiarizing yourself with the study passage, reading it, and answering the study questions. Consider the **Study Summary**, **Athlete Connection**, and **Keys to Winning**. Go to the group study ready to participate, ask questions, provide insight, seek help, and sharpen your fellow athletes in their pursuit of Christ.

Encourage one another throughout the week with the truths you are learning. As iron sharpens iron, so one athlete will sharpen another.

Trust God to do a powerful work in your heart and life. The Word of God is living and active, sharper than a two-edged sword. It pierces to the division of soul and spirit, joints, and marrow, and discerns the thoughts and intentions of the heart. It will do heart surgery on you if you surrender yourself to it. So, give yourself to this study and watch God work powerfully in and through you in the details of your athletics and personal life.

Read the Scouting Report prior to Week One. Just as you try to know as much as you can about your opponent before you play them, you need to know as much as you can about the context of Colossians before you study it.

Don't worry if you can't find another athlete to study with you. The best way to profit from this study is with a group of other athletes, but you can certainly do it on your own. If you're a Christian, you have the Spirit of Christ living in you. He will give you illumination along the way. So don't let your isolation from other like-minded athletes discourage you. We encourage you to ask your local pastor, FCA staff, or church leader to walk through it with you. Anyone who loves the Lord and wants to grow into greater maturity could be a great study partner.

SCOUTING REPORT

ON COLOSSIANS

The TITLE of Colossians

- The title "Colossians" refers to the recipients of the letter, the Christians in the city of Colossae. Situated in Asia Minor (modern-day Turkey), Colossae was a relatively small city with a growing church that had been established through the ministry of Epaphras, a co-laborer of the Apostle Paul. Though Paul had never personally visited the Colossian church, he wrote this letter to address their specific needs, including the threat of false teachings undermining the sufficiency of Christ. The title highlights the personal nature of Paul's communication, directed at a community of believers striving to live out their faith amidst cultural challenges. Through this letter, Paul exhorts the Colossians to grow in spiritual maturity, reminding them that Christ is preeminent over all creation and fully sufficient for their salvation and sanctification.

The AUTHORSHIP of Colossians

- The Apostle Paul is the author, as stated in the opening verse of the letter (Colossians 1:1). Written during Paul's imprisonment, likely in Rome around AD 60-62, this epistle is part of what is known as the "Prison Letters," along with Ephesians, Philippians, and Philemon. Paul's deep theological insight, pastoral care, and commitment to the gospel are evident throughout the letter, as he combats false teachings threatening the church and points the believers back to the sufficiency and supremacy of Christ. His passion for presenting believers as "mature in Christ" (Colossians 1:28) reflects the heart of his ministry and mission, which was to see the church strengthened and growing in faith.

The CENTRAL THEME of Colossians

- The theme of spiritual maturity is woven throughout the book of Colossians, as Paul continually emphasizes the believers' need to grow in their understanding and relationship with Christ. Paul frequently uses words like "full," "all," and "every" to express his desire for the Colossians to not just know Christ in part, but to know Him in full and be made complete in Him. In Colossians 1:9-10, Paul prays that they would be "filled with the knowledge of His will in all spiritual wisdom and understanding" and "bear fruit in every good work." Later, in Colossians 2:9-10, he declares that "in Christ all the fullness of the Deity lives in bodily form," and that believers "have been given fullness in Christ." This fullness and completeness are key aspects of spiritual maturity, which Paul aims for when he says his goal is to "present everyone fully mature in Christ" (Colossians 1:28). Paul understands that true maturity can only happen by looking to Christ, the source of all wisdom and knowledge, and living in light of His preeminence and sufficiency. The Colossians are called to reject false teachings and grow into full maturity by deepening their faith and understanding of Christ, who alone can make them complete.

The STRUCTURE of Colossians

- Introduction and Thanksgiving (1:1-14)

  a. Greeting and Salutation (1:1-2)
    - ~ Paul introduces himself as the author and addresses the saints in Colossae.
    - ~ Paul includes Timothy in his greeting.

  b. Thanksgiving and Prayer for Spiritual Growth (1:3-14)
    - ~Paul expresses gratitude for the Colossians' faith, love, and hope.
    - ~He prays for their continued growth in knowledge, wisdom, and strength.
    - ~He highlights their deliverance and redemption in Christ.

- The Supremacy and Sufficiency of Christ (1:15-2:7)

  a. The Preeminence of Christ (1:15-20)
    - ~ Christ's role in creation and His preeminence over all things.
    - ~ Christ as the head of the church and the agent of reconciliation.

  b. Reconciliation through Christ (1:21-23)
    - ~ The Colossians are reconciled to God through Christ's death.
    - ~ Paul exhorts them to remain steadfast in the faith.

  c. Paul's Ministry for the Maturity of the Church (1:24-29)
    - ~ Paul's sufferings are for the church's growth and maturity.
    - ~ His labor is to present everyone fully mature in Christ.

  d. Encouragement to Walk in Christ (2:1-7)
    - ~ Paul expresses his concern for the spiritual well-being of the Colossians.
    - ~ He encourages them to walk in Christ, rooted and built up in Him, strengthened in faith.

- Warnings Against False Teachings (2:8-23)

a. Rejecting Empty Philosophy (2:8-10)

~ Paul warns against deceptive philosophies and human traditions.

~ He emphasizes that all fullness dwells in Christ, and believers are complete in Him.

b. The Fullness of Christ's Work (2:11-15)

~ Paul explains the spiritual circumcision believers experience in Christ.

~ Christ's victory over sin and spiritual powers through the cross.

c. Freedom from Legalism (2:16-17)

~ Paul warns against legalistic judgments related to food, festivals, and Sabbath observance.

~ These are shadows; the reality is found in Christ.

d. Avoiding False Asceticism (2:18-23)

~ Paul warns against ascetic practices and false humility.

~ Such regulations appear wise but lack value in restraining sinful behavior.

- **The Christian Life: Putting on the New Self (3:1-4:6)**

a. Seek the Things Above (3:1-4)

~ Paul exhorts believers to set their hearts and minds on things above, not earthly things.

~ Their lives are hidden with Christ, awaiting His glorious return.

b. Putting Off the Old Self (3:5-11)

~ Believers are called to put to death sinful behaviors such as sexual immorality, anger, and slander.

~ The old self is replaced by the new self, renewed in knowledge after the image of Christ.

c. Putting On the New Self (3:12-17)

~ Paul exhorts the Colossians to clothe themselves with virtues like compassion, kindness, humility, and love.

~ The peace of Christ and the word of Christ should govern their lives as they live in gratitude.

d. Christ-Centered Relationships (3:18-4:1)

~Instructions for households: Wives, husbands, children, and fathers are called to Christlike relationships.

~ Slaves and masters are given instructions on how to serve and lead in a Christ-honoring way.

e. Prayer and Wise Living (4:2-6)

~ Paul calls for a devoted prayer life, praying for opportunities to proclaim the Gospel.

~ Believers are exhorted to live wisely before outsiders and to make the most of every opportunity.

- Final Greetings and Instructions (4:7-18)

a. Commendation of Paul's Coworkers (4:7-14)

~ Paul sends greetings from his fellow workers, including Tychicus, Onesimus, Aristarchus, and others.

~ He highlights their faithful service and their concern for the Colossian church.

b. Instructions to the Church (4:15-17)

~ Paul instructs the Colossians to share this letter with the Laodiceans and mentions his personal requests.

~ He encourages Archippus to fulfill his ministry.

c. Paul's Closing Words (4:18)

~ Paul concludes with a personal signature, a reminder of his imprisonment, and a final blessing.

The STUDY of Colossians

How should we read and study Colossians today? When reading and studying Colossians today, we should approach it with a desire to deepen our understanding of Christ's supremacy and sufficiency, recognizing that Paul's call to spiritual maturity is just as relevant now as it was then. As we study, it's essential to reflect on how we can put off our old, sinful nature and actively put on the virtues of Christ, allowing His Word to shape our character, relationships, and daily actions. Colossians also challenges us to remain vigilant against modern "philosophies" and influences that undermine the Gospel, reminding us that we are complete in Christ alone. Ultimately, studying Colossians should lead to a deeper appreciation for the fullness of life found in Christ, encouraging us to grow in wisdom, faith, and devotion as we pursue spiritual maturity and live out our calling as followers of Jesus.

PREGAME QUESTIONS

1. **When you think of spiritual maturity, what comes to your mind?** What qualities, habits, or attitudes do you associate with being mature in your faith, both in your personal life and as an athlete?

_____

_____

_____

_____

_____

_____

2. **Athletes often focus on developing physically, but how often do they consider their spiritual growth?** How can athletics go beyond physical training to include developing character and spiritual maturity?

_____

_____

_____

_____

_____

_____

3. **What are some competing "philosophies" or influences that can distract you from fully relying on Christ?** How do you think Colossians speaks to these distractions?

_____

_____

_____

_____

_____

_____

4. **At the end of this study in 12 weeks, what would you like to see God do in your heart?** What specific areas of growth do you hope to experience as an athlete and follower of Christ?

_____

_____

_____

_____

_____

_____

5. **Colossians emphasizes being "rooted and built up in Christ" (Col. 2:7).** What does it mean for you to be "rooted" in Christ as an athlete, and how does that influence how you interact with others?

_____

_____

_____

_____

_____

_____

_____

6. **Think of a teammate who could be a partner in this study for mutual accountability, encouragement, and prayer.** Will you commit to walking through this study with them, holding each other accountable for growth in Christ and maturity as leaders? Write their name below and plan how you will support each other weekly.

_____

_____

_____

_____

_____

_____

_____

NOTES:

★ ★ ★

CHAPTER ONE
THE COMPLETE ATHLETE
REJOICES IN MATURITY

COLOSSIANS 1:1-8

STUDY STARTER

Tim Tebow, former NFL quarterback and now a sports broadcaster, is a great example of a Christian athlete who finds joy in the process of spiritual growth. Known for his outspoken faith, Tebow's story is full of incredible highs and challenging lows. He became a household name at the University of Florida, where he won the Heisman Trophy, but his NFL career was not as smooth. Though he had early success, especially with the Denver Broncos, he also faced plenty of criticism. Through it all, Tebow stayed grounded in his faith, using every opportunity to spread hope, love, and purpose.

When his playing days started winding down, Tebow didn't let that stop him. Instead, he stepped into new roles that showed how much he'd grown—not just as an athlete but as a Christian. He became a commentator, author, and philanthropist, pouring his energy into the Tim Tebow Foundation. The foundation focuses on helping kids in need and fighting poverty, giving Tebow a platform to serve others in a big way. While many athletes struggle to find joy after their careers peak, Tebow found even greater fulfillment by living out his faith and focusing on helping others.

Tebow's growth shines through in how he talks about his faith and how it's guided him through both successes and setbacks. He's shared in interviews that true success isn't about wins and losses but about making a positive impact on others through love and kindness. In his book Shaken, Tebow opens up about his journey and encourages readers to stay faithful through tough times. By focusing on purpose and service—whether through his foundation, writing, or public speaking—Tebow shows that real joy isn't about athletic accomplishments but about living a life that reflects Christ's love.

Tebow's joy in his maturing faith reflects the heart of Paul's message to the Colossians. Paul expresses gratitude for the believers' faith, love, and maturity in the gospel, celebrating the growth he sees in their spiritual lives. Paul rejoices in the spiritual maturity of the Colossian church, recognizing that their progress is evidence of God's work within them and desiring for them to excel still more. This study should remind us that growth—whether in faith, character, or relationships—is worth celebrating, as it reflects God's ongoing work in our lives and others. Through Tebow's example and Paul's words, we are encouraged to find joy in the growth of others and in our own journey toward maturity.

STUDY PASSAGE

1 Paul, an apostle of Christ Jesus by the will of God, and Timothy our brother, ² To the saints and faithful brothers in Christ at Colossae: Grace to you and peace from God our Father. ³ We always thank God, the Father of our Lord Jesus Christ, when we pray for you, ⁴ since we heard of your faith in Christ Jesus and of the love that you have for all the saints, ⁵ because of the hope laid up for you in heaven. Of this you have heard before in the word of the truth, the gospel, ⁶ which has come to you, as indeed in the whole world it is bearing fruit and increasing—as it also does among you, since the day you heard it and understood the grace of God in truth, ⁷ just as you learned it from Epaphras our beloved fellow servant. He is a faithful minister of Christ on your behalf ⁸ and has made known to us your love in the Spirit. (ESV)

STUDY HELP

- **"thankfulness"**—In Colossians 1:3, Paul expresses his thankfulness for the faith, love, and hope of the Colossian believers. Thankfulness is a theme in Paul's writings, reflecting his deep gratitude to God for the work He is doing in the lives of others. In this passage, Paul models how Christian leaders should cultivate an attitude of thankfulness, recognizing that the growth and fruitfulness in others' lives are ultimately the result of God's grace. This gratitude is not just a polite acknowledgment but a foundational posture of the heart, acknowledging God's ongoing work of transformation in believers.

- **"hope"**—Paul speaks of the "hope laid up for you in heaven" (Colossians 1:5), highlighting the future-oriented confidence that anchors the believers' faith and love. In the Bible, hope is more than a vague wish—it's a confident expectation rooted in God's promises. For the Colossians, this hope fuels their perseverance and shapes their daily lives as they look forward to the fulfillment of God's ultimate plan in Christ. This hope isn't limited to earthly successes or circumstances but is firmly secured in the eternal promises of God. For believers, hope offers motivation and endurance, knowing that the challenges of this life are temporary and that their ultimate reward is with Christ.

- *"word of truth"*—In Colossians 1:5, Paul refers to the "word of truth, the gospel" as the life-transforming message that has come to the Colossians and continues to bear fruit throughout the world. The "word of truth" is the gospel of Jesus Christ— God's revelation of salvation through His Son, which stands in stark contrast to the false teachings that were creeping into the Colossian church. This phrase emphasizes the reliability and power of the gospel to change lives and bring people to maturity in Christ.

STUDY QUESTIONS

1. In verses 3-4, Paul expresses thankfulness for the Colossians' faith and love. Why do you think Paul emphasizes these two qualities, and how are they connected to spiritual maturity in Christ?

_____

_____

_____

_____

2. Paul mentions that the Colossians' faith and love are rooted in the "hope laid up for you in heaven" (v. 5). How does the hope of eternal life influence the way you live now? In what ways does your understanding of heavenly hope affect your actions and priorities in your daily life?

_____

_____

_____

_____

3. In verse 5, Paul calls the gospel "the word of truth." What do you think Paul means by this phrase, and how does the truth of the gospel contrast with the false teachings threatening the Colossian church?

_____

_____

_____

_____

4. In verse 6, Paul says that the gospel is "bearing fruit and growing" throughout the world. What does it mean for the gospel to bear fruit, both globally and personally?

_____

_____

_____

_____

5. Paul acknowledges Epaphras' role in bringing the gospel to the Colossians (v. 7). What can we learn from Epaphras' faithfulness in sharing the gospel?

_____

_____

_____

_____

6. Verses 3-8 emphasize the interconnectedness of faith, love, and hope. How do these three qualities work together in the life of a believer? Which of these areas do you feel most called to grow in, and how can you cultivate that growth in your daily walk with Christ?

_____

_____

_____

_____

STUDY SUMMARY

Colossians 1:1-8 introduces Paul's letter with a focus on thankfulness for the Colossians' faith in Christ, love for others, and the hope they have in heaven. Paul highlights the transformative power of the gospel, which is bearing fruit globally and in their lives, urging them to remain rooted in these foundational truths as they continue to grow spiritually.

ATHLETE CONNECTION

The complete athlete rejoices in the personal achievements and spiritual maturity of those they influence, celebrating the gospel's transformative work in their lives. This passage encourages athletes to focus on nurturing the whole person, finding fulfillment in the growth and development as they become more rooted in Christ.

KEYS TO WINNING

▶ **VIDEO GUIDE AT KINGDOMSPORTS.ONLINE**

▶ THANKFULNESS FOR SPIRITUAL GROWTH

Paul expresses deep gratitude for the faith, love, and hope evident in the Colossians' lives, reminding us to be thankful for the spiritual growth and maturity we see in others.

How often do you take the time to thank God for the spiritual growth you see in those around you, whether teammates, colleagues, or those you lead? Reflect on a specific instance where you've seen someone grow in faith, love, or hope—how did you respond, and how can you cultivate a heart of thankfulness for such moments?

_____

_____

_____

2. Reflect on a specific instance where you've seen someone grow in faith, love, or hope—how did you respond, and how can you cultivate a heart of thankfulness for such moments?

_____

_____

_____

_____

▶ THE TRANSFORMING POWER OF THE GOSPEL

The gospel is described as "bearing fruit and growing" both in Colossae and around the world, highlighting its ongoing transformative power in the lives of believers.

1. How have you personally experienced the transforming power of the gospel in your life, and how is it continuing to bear fruit in your daily actions and relationships?

_____

_____

_____

_____

2. In what ways are you actively allowing the gospel to "grow and bear fruit" through your influence on others, whether in your family, team, or community? Consider how you can further share the gospel's transformative power, helping others experience spiritual growth and maturity.

_____

_____

_____

_____

▶ THE IMPORTANCE OF FAITH, LOVE, AND HOPE

These three foundational virtues—faith in Christ, love for others, and hope in the promises of God—are central to the Christian life and a key focus for personal and communal spiritual maturity.

1. Which of these three virtues—faith, love, or hope—do you feel is strongest in your life right now, and which one do you feel needs further growth?

_____

_____

_____

_____

2. How are you actively cultivating faith, love, and hope in those you influence, whether in your personal life, team, or church?

_____

_____

_____

_____

GAME CHANGER

Paul begins his letter with a spirit of gratitude for the faith, love, and hope evident in the Colossian believers' lives. This passage reminds us of the importance of recognizing the spiritual growth in others and ourselves. Just as Paul rejoiced in seeing these virtues flourish in the Colossians, we should also cultivate a heart of thankfulness for the work God is doing in and through His people. By focusing on these qualities—faith in Christ, love for others, and hope in the promises of God—we are encouraged to reflect on how these virtues shape our daily lives and relationships.

The gospel is central to this transformation. Paul notes that the "word of truth, the gospel," is bearing fruit and growing, both in Colossae and around the world. This ongoing growth reminds us that the gospel is not a static message but an active and powerful force that continues to change lives. When we open ourselves to the gospel's work, we experience its transformative power—leading us to deeper faith, genuine love for others, and an unshakable hope in the future God has promised. The gospel doesn't just bring salvation; it fosters ongoing spiritual maturity, molding us more into the image of Christ.

Ultimately, Colossians 1:1-8 points us back to the heart of the gospel, reminding us that all spiritual growth comes through Christ. We are called to rely fully on Him, knowing He is the source of our faith, love, and hope. As we grow in these areas, we bear witness to the power of the gospel, allowing its fruit to be visible in our lives. This passage challenges us to stay rooted in Christ, to be thankful for His work, and to live in a way that reflects the transformative message of the gospel to those around us.

ONE BIG THING

What is the most significant lesson for you to take with you from these verses?

_____

_____

_____

_____

_____

_____

_____

_____

_____

IMPACT PRAYER

Heavenly Father, thank You for the powerful reminder in Colossians of the faith, love, and hope You cultivate in us through the gospel. Help us to recognize and rejoice in the spiritual growth happening in our lives and in the lives of others. May we always be thankful for the work You are doing, shaping us into the image of Christ. As the gospel continues to bear fruit in the world, let it transform our hearts and deepen our faith, love, and hope. Keep us rooted in You. Amen

NOTES:

★ ★ ★

CHAPTER TWO
THE COMPLETE ATHLETE
PRAYS FOR MATURITY

COLOSSIANS 1:9-14

STUDY STARTER

One of the most inspiring stories of an athlete praying for maturity is that of Derrick Coleman, the former NFL fullback who lost his hearing as a child. Derrick faced huge challenges growing up—he was often teased because of his hearing loss and struggled to fit in. As he worked his way up in football, the obstacles didn't stop. He had to constantly prove himself, not just because of his disability but because of the pressure to show he belonged. Early in his career, Derrick admitted to being impatient and quick-tempered, frustrated by feeling misunderstood or underestimated. He eventually realized that raw talent wasn't enough—if he wanted a lasting career in the NFL, he needed emotional and spiritual growth.

Things hit a low point during a tough season when Derrick started doubting himself. That's when he leaned into his faith. Known for being open about his Christian beliefs, Derrick often talked about how prayer helped keep him grounded. After a particularly rough game where he felt he let his team down, he didn't pray for fame or success. Instead, he asked God for wisdom and maturity. He prayed for patience to face challenges, grace to handle adversity, and strength that went beyond physical ability. Derrick wanted to be more than just a good player—he wanted to be a role model, especially for kids with disabilities who saw him as an example.

That prayer became a turning point. Derrick started approaching football—and life—with more humility and a stronger sense of responsibility. His faith and perseverance helped him navigate injuries, setbacks, and the constant pressure of playing in the NFL. Off the field, he became a passionate advocate for the hearing-impaired community, using his platform to inspire and support others. Derrick often said in interviews that prayer and his relationship with God gave him the strength to grow into a better athlete and person. His journey is a powerful example of how faith, perseverance, and humility can transform a career and a life.

As we study Colossians 1:9-14, we see Derrick's prayer for maturity marked a turning point in his career and life. It serves to provide a powerful illustration of Paul's prayer for the Colossian church. Paul asks that the believers be "filled with the knowledge of His will," strengthened with patience and endurance, and overflowing with gratitude. Similarly, Derrick began approaching the game and his teammates with a renewed sense of humility and responsibility. His perseverance and faith carried him through obstacles, including injuries and pressure to play at the highest level. This study invites us to consider the importance of praying not only for our own needs or physical needs but, most importantly, for the spiritual growth of those around us, seeking God's guidance and strength in our collective journey of faith.

STUDY PASSAGE

1 *⁹ And so, from the day we heard, we have not ceased to pray for you, asking that you may be filled with the knowledge of his will in all spiritual wisdom and understanding, ¹⁰ so as to walk in a manner worthy of the Lord, fully pleasing to him: bearing fruit in every good work and increasing in the knowledge of God; ¹¹ being strengthened with all power, according to his glorious might, for all endurance and patience with joy; ¹²] giving thanks to the Father, who has qualified you to share in the inheritance of the saints in light. ¹³ He has delivered us from the domain of darkness and transferred us to the kingdom of his beloved Son, ¹⁴ in whom we have redemption, the forgiveness of sins. (ESV)*

STUDY HELP

- *"knowledge"*—In verse 9, Paul prays that the Colossians may be filled with the "knowledge of His will." In the book of Colossians, the Apostle Paul emphasizes the concept of "knowledge," particularly the knowledge of God's will and the knowledge of Christ Himself. This emphasis serves as a foundation for spiritual maturity and safeguards against false teachings infiltrating the church in Colossae.

- *"wisdom"*—Paul emphasizes "wisdom" as a crucial component of spiritual maturity and a safeguard against false teachings. Wisdom, in Paul's context, is not merely human intellect or philosophical reasoning but divine insight granted by God through the Holy Spirit.

- *"redemption"*—The term "redemption" refers to the act of being set free from bondage through the payment of a ransom. In Colossians, Paul weaves this theme to highlight the sufficiency of Christ's sacrifice and its implications for spiritual maturity and daily living.

STUDY QUESTIONS

1. In verse 9, Paul prays that the Colossians may be "filled with the knowledge of His will in all spiritual wisdom and understanding." What does it mean to be "filled with the knowledge of His will" and how do "spiritual wisdom and understanding" differ from worldly wisdom, and why are they important for spiritual maturity?

_____

_____

_____

_____

2. How can we live a life worthy of the Lord and please Him in every way, bearing fruit in every good work and growing in the knowledge of God, as emphasized in verse 10?

_____

_____

_____

_____

3. Why is it essential for believers to be strengthened with all power according to His glorious might, as mentioned in verse 11, and how does this enable us to exhibit endurance and patience in challenging situations?

_____

_____

_____

_____

4. What does it mean that God has "qualified" us to share in the inheritance of His holy people, as stated in verses 12-14, and how does understanding our inheritance inspire gratitude and influence the way we live)?

_____

_____

_____

_____

5. How does being rescued from the dominion of darkness and brought into the kingdom of the Son He loves, as described in verse 13, change our perspective on life, and in what ways does recognizing our transfer into Christ's kingdom affect our priorities and goals?

_____

_____

_____

_____

6. Considering that this passage highlights themes of spiritual growth, transformation, and gratitude, how does Paul's prayer model how we should pray for ourselves and others regarding spiritual maturity, and how does embracing these principles influence your approach to personal development?

_____

_____

_____

_____

STUDY SUMMARY

In Colossians 1:9-14, Paul prays for the Colossians to be filled with the knowledge of God's will through spiritual wisdom and understanding, so they may live lives worthy of the Lord, bearing fruit in every good work and growing in the knowledge of God. He emphasizes the importance of being strengthened with God's power to endure with patience and joyfully give thanks to the Father, who has qualified them to share in the inheritance of the saints by delivering them from darkness and redeeming them through His Son..

ATHLETE CONNECTION

The complete athlete deeply understands God's will through spiritual wisdom in Scripture, lives a life worthy of the Lord by bearing fruit in good works, and continually grows in the knowledge of God. Relying on God's strength, the athlete exhibits endurance and patience, maintains a joyful and thankful heart, and exhibiting integrity, inspiring spiritual growth while navigating challenges with divine guidance and gratitude.

KEYS TO WINNING

▶ VIDEO GUIDE AT KINGDOMSPORTS.ONLINE

▶ THE IMPORTANCE OF KNOWING GOD'S WILL

Paul prays for the Colossians to be filled with the knowledge of God's will through all spiritual wisdom and understanding (verse 9). This emphasizes that spiritual maturity begins with a deep understanding of God's desires and purposes. Knowing God's will enables believers to align their lives with His plans and designs.

1. How are you intentionally seeking to be filled with the knowledge of God's will through spiritual wisdom and understanding in your daily life?

_____

_____

_____

_____

2. In what areas of your life do you feel closely aligned with God's plans, and where might there be misalignment or uncertainty about His will?

_____

_____

_____

_____

▶ LIVING A LIFE WORTHY OF THE LORD

The passage highlights that understanding God's will should result in action—living a life worthy of the Lord and pleasing Him in every way (verse 10). This includes bearing fruit in every good work and growing in the knowledge of God. It underscores the connection between knowledge and practice, showing that true understanding manifests in ethical behavior and continual spiritual growth.

1. In what areas of your life do you feel you are effectively living a life worthy of the Lord, bearing fruit in good works, and where might you need to improve to align more closely with His will?

_____

_____

_____

_____

2. How does your understanding of God's will translate into practical actions in your daily life, and what steps can you take to ensure that your knowledge leads to ethical behavior and spiritual growth?

_____

_____

_____

_____

3. What disciplines or routines can you establish to continue growing in the knowledge of God, and how might this ongoing growth influence the way you live and interact with others?

_____

_____

_____

_____

▶ STRENGTH AND ENDURANCE THROUGH GOD'S POWER

Paul emphasizes the need to be strengthened with all power according to God's glorious might so believers may have great endurance and patience (verse 11). This takeaway reminds us that spiritual strength and the ability to persevere through challenges come from relying on God's power rather than our own. It encourages maintaining a joyful and thankful heart, recognizing that God has rescued and brought us into His kingdom (verses 12-14).

1. In which areas of your life are you relying on your own strength instead of seeking God's power for endurance and patience?

_____

_____

_____

_____

2. How does recognizing that God has rescued and brought you into His kingdom influence you to maintain a joyful and thankful heart during difficult times?

_____

_____

_____

_____

GAME CHANGER

The Apostle Paul offers a heartfelt prayer for believers to be filled with the knowledge of God's will through all spiritual wisdom and understanding. This passage invites the reader to go beyond mere intellectual acknowledgment. By earnestly knowing and pursuing God's revealed will in Scripture, we align ourselves with His divine purpose, allowing His wisdom to guide our decisions and actions. This alignment transforms our daily walk, enabling us to live lives worthy of the Lord, bearing fruit in every good work and growing continuously in our knowledge of Him.

As we are strengthened with all power according to His glorious might, we develop great endurance and patience. Divine strength is not something we muster on our own; it is a gracious gift from God that empowers us to overcome obstacles with a joyful and thankful heart. Recognizing that we have been qualified to share in this inheritance it should fill us with gratitude and reinforce our identity as beloved children of God. This gratitude propels us to live out our faith authentically, reflecting God's love and grace to those around us.

This passage is a reminder of the power of the gospel—the good news of Jesus Christ. God has rescued us from the dominion of darkness and brought us into the kingdom of His beloved Son, in whom we have redemption and the forgiveness of sins. This rescue is at the heart of the gospel message: through Jesus' sacrifice, we are redeemed and restored to a right relationship with God. Understanding this truth transforms our perspective as we realize that our ability to know God's will, live worthy lives, and be strengthened by His power is made possible through Christ's redemptive work.

ONE BIG THING

What is the most significant lesson for you to take with you from this chapter?

_____

_____

_____

_____

_____

_____

_____

_____

IMPACT PRAYER

Heavenly Father, thank You for filling us with the knowledge of Your will through all spiritual wisdom and understanding. Help us align with Your divine purpose, guiding our decisions so we may live lives worthy of You, bearing fruit in every good work. Strengthen us with Your glorious might, granting us endurance and patience, and fill our hearts with gratitude for rescuing us through the redemption and forgiveness found in Jesus Christ. In Jesus' name, Amen.

★ ★ ★

CHAPTER THREE
THE COMPLETE ATHLETE
EXALTS CHRIST

COLOSSIANS 1:15-20

STUDY STARTER

Kurt Warner, a former NFL quarterback, is famous not just for his incredible story of going from undrafted free agent to Super Bowl MVP but also for how openly he shared his faith throughout his career. After not getting drafted in 1994, Warner hit some major roadblocks. He worked at a grocery store and played in the Arena Football League, but through it all, he leaned on his relationship with Christ. Warner often said his faith gave him the strength and patience to trust that God had a different plan for his life.

Everything changed when Warner got his big break and led the St. Louis Rams to a win in Super Bowl XXXIV, where he also earned MVP honors. During post-game interviews, he made it clear who he credited for his success, famously saying, "First things first, I've got to thank my Lord and Savior up above—thank you, Jesus!" That kind of public acknowledgment became a signature part of his career. Warner saw his success as a chance to share his faith, often pointing to God as the reason for his achievements and expressing deep gratitude.

Off the field, Warner and his wife, Brenda, started the First Things First Foundation, which focuses on helping people in need while promoting Christian values. The foundation supports causes like children's hospitals, single parents, and individuals with developmental disabilities. Warner's commitment to faith and service didn't go unnoticed—he received awards like the Walter Payton NFL Man of the Year, which recognizes both charity work and on-field excellence. Through it all, Kurt Warner has shown how an athlete can use their platform to exalt Christ, integrating faith into every part of their life and career.

Warner's life mirrors the message of Colossians 1:15-20, where Christ is exalted as the Creator, Sustainer, and the One in whom "all things hold together." Just as this passage calls believers to see Christ as supreme in every aspect, Warner's journey illustrates a life centered on exalting Christ. His actions, both in his athletic career and philanthropic efforts, reflect a deep desire to honor Jesus in every opportunity. For Warner, faith is not just part of his identity—it is his foundation, shaping everything he does and serving as a powerful example of what it means to worship Christ fully in every sphere of life.

STUDY PASSAGE

1 [15] *He is the image of the invisible God, the firstborn of all creation.* [16] *For by him all things were created, in heaven and on earth, visible and invisible, whether thrones or dominions or rulers or authorities—all things were created through him and for him.* [17] *And he is before all things, and in him all things hold together.* [18] *And he is the head of the body, the church. He is the beginning, the firstborn from the dead, that in everything he might be preeminent.* [19] *For in him all the fullness of God was pleased to dwell,* [20] *and through him to reconcile to himself all things, whether on earth or in heaven, making peace by the blood of his cross. (ESV).*

STUDY HELP

- *"image"*— This word emphasizes that Jesus perfectly represents and reveals the nature of God to humanity. Studying "image" helps you understand the concept of Christ being the visible manifestation of the invisible God, which is central to grasping His divinity and role in salvation.

- *"firstborn"*—The term "firstborn" signifies supremacy and preeminence rather than chronological birth order. Exploring this word allows you to delve into Christ's authority over all creation and His unique status as supreme above all things, highlighting His eternal existence and sovereignty.

- *"fullness"*—"Fullness" indicates that the complete nature and essence of God reside in Christ. Highlighting this word helps you comprehend the completeness of Christ's deity and how He embodies all the attributes of God, reinforcing the doctrine of the Trinity.

STUDY QUESTIONS

1. What does it mean that Christ is "the image of the invisible God" (verse 15)? How does this concept help us understand the nature of God and His revelation to humanity through Jesus?

_____

_____

_____

_____

2. How should you interpret the term "firstborn over all creation" (verse 15)? What are the implications of this title for understanding Christ's authority over all things?

_____

_____

_____

_____

3. What is the significance of all things being created "through Him and for Him" (verse 16)? How does recognizing Christ as the agent and purpose of creation affect our view of the world and our place in it?

_____

_____

_____

_____

4. How does Christ "hold all things together," and what does this reveal about His ongoing relationship with creation?

_____

_____

_____

_____

5. What does it mean that Christ is "the head of the body, the church" and "the beginning and the firstborn from among the dead" (verse 18)?

_____

_____

_____

_____

6. Why was God pleased to have "all His fullness dwell in Him" and to "reconcile to Himself all things" through Christ and what are the implications for believers?

_____

_____

_____

_____

STUDY SUMMARY

Colossians 1:15-20 proclaims the supremacy and deity of Jesus Christ, stating that He is the image of the invisible God and the firstborn over all creation. This passage emphasizes that all things were created through Him and for Him, and through His fullness, God reconciled all things to Himself, highlighting Christ's central role in creation and redemption.

ATHLETE CONNECTION

The complete athlete proclaims the supremacy and full deity of Jesus Christ, emphasizing that He is the image of the invisible God and the creator and sustainer of all things. This means placing Christ at the center of your athletic philosophy, modeling His character in your interactions, and relying on His guidance to lead.

KEYS TO WINNING

▶ VIDEO GUIDE AT KINGDOMSPORTS.ONLINE

▶ THE SUPREMACY AND PREEMINENCE OF CHRIST IN CREATION

Recognizing the supremacy and preeminence of Christ means placing Jesus at the center of your athletic philosophy and practice. Understanding that all things were created through Him and for Him (Colossians 1:16) instructs you to align your goals and methods with His purposes. This perspective transforms athletics into a form of worship, where every training session, game, and interaction becomes an opportunity to honor Christ.

1. How can you intentionally place Jesus at the center of your athletic philosophy and daily practice, recognizing His supremacy and preeminence in all things?

_____

_____

_____

_____

2. In what ways does understanding that all things were created through Him and for Him influence your approach to setting goals and interacting with your team and others?

_____

_____

_____

_____

▶ CHRIST AS THE SUSTAINER AND HEAD OF THE CHURCH

Knowing that Christ is before all things and that in Him all things hold together provides a foundation of trust and reliance on His sustaining power. You can find confidence and peace in the fact that Jesus is the ultimate leader—the head of the body, the church

(Colossians 1:18). This understanding encourages you to depend on His wisdom and strength rather than solely on your abilities.

1. How does recognizing that Christ is before all things and that in Him all things hold together influence your trust and reliance on His sustaining power? Reflect on specific areas where you may have been relying primarily on your own abilities.

_____

_____

_____

_____

2. In what ways can acknowledging Jesus as the ultimate leader—the head of the body, the church—bring confidence and peace to your role as the complete athlete, and how might this understanding impact your interactions with your team?

_____

_____

_____

_____

▶ THE FULLNESS OF GOD DWELLING IN CHRIST AND RECONCILIATION TO GOD THROUGH HIM

Embracing the truth that all the fullness of God dwells in Christ and that through Him, God reconciles all things empowers you to be an ambassador of reconciliation in your athletic role. Recognizing the completeness and sufficiency of Christ's sacrifice motivates you to foster an environment of grace, forgiveness, and restoration within your team. When conflicts arise, you can lead by example in pursuing peace and facilitating healing conversations.

1. How does the understanding that all the fullness of God dwells in Christ and that He reconciles all things to Himself inspire you to promote grace, forgiveness, and restoration in relationships?

_____

_____

_____

_____

2. In what practical ways can you be an ambassador of reconciliation in your life, especially during times of tension or disagreement?

_____

_____

_____

_____

GAME CHANGER

Colossians 1:15-20 reveals Christ's supremacy and centrality in creation and redemption, proclaiming that Jesus is "the image of the invisible God" and the one in whom "all things hold together." This truth calls us to recognize Jesus not only as a historical figure but as the sovereign Lord who intimately sustains all of creation. For each of us, this understanding transforms our daily lives, reminding us that everything—our work, relationships, challenges, and achievements—finds its purpose and cohesion in Him. Knowing that Christ holds all things together reassures us in uncertain times, anchoring our trust in His sustaining power rather than in fleeting circumstances.

As the "firstborn over all creation," Christ is not only supreme over the world but also the head of the church, leading us in spiritual growth and unity. His role as head shapes how we approach our relationships, calling us to reflect His character in every interaction and to pursue lives that honor Him. This passage challenges us to see our lives as a reflection of His love and grace, demonstrating humility, patience, and forgiveness as we strive to live out our faith. By aligning our lives with His example, we become conduits of His peace, fostering reconciliation and unity in our families, communities, and workplaces.

God has reconciled all things to Himself, making peace through Christ's shed blood on the cross. This reconciliation changes everything—it means that no sin or failure can separate us from God's love. Embracing this gospel truth invites us to live with gratitude, knowing that Christ's all-sufficient sacrifice has secured our peace with God. As we grasp the fullness of God dwelling in Christ and His reconciling power, we are inspired to live boldly, letting His love and grace shape every aspect of our lives.

ONE BIG THING

What is the most significant lesson for you to take with you from this chapter?

_____

_____

_____

_____

_____

_____

_____

_____

_____

_____

_____

_____

_____

_____

_____

_____

_____

IMPACT PRAYER

Lord Jesus, we praise You as the image of the invisible God, the one who holds all things together and leads us in peace and unity. Help us to recognize Your supreme place in every part of our lives and to live with hearts anchored in Your sustaining power, especially in uncertain times. Thank You for reconciling us to the Father through Your sacrifice, bringing us peace and purpose. May we reflect Your love, grace, and humility in our interactions, living boldly and gratefully for You. In Your name, we pray, Amen.

★ ★ ★

CHAPTER FOUR
THE COMPLETE ATHLETE

REMAINS STEADFAST

COLOSSIANS 1:21-23

STUDY STARTER

Olympic gold medalist Allyson Felix is a great example of an athlete staying grounded in her faith. Known as one of the best sprinters in history, Felix has always been open about her relationship with Christ. Early on, people called her the "Chicken Legs" sprinter because of her slim build, but Felix didn't let that shake her confidence. Instead, she leaned on her faith, often saying, "My faith motivates me. My faith is the reason I run." Throughout her career, Felix faced tough challenges like injuries and setbacks, but she consistently turned to God for guidance and peace.

One of her hardest moments came when she took on Nike over how they treated female athletes who became moms. After having her daughter in 2018 through an emergency C-section, Felix became an advocate for better maternity protections. She openly shared how her faith helped her stay strong during these trials, trusting that standing up for her values was the right thing to do, even at the cost of professional relationships. Felix stated that she believed God placed her in a position to advocate for other women and to glorify Him by staying true to her convictions.

Even with all the pressure of competition and advocacy, Felix kept pointing to Christ in everything she did. In her final Olympics in 2021, she became the most decorated U.S. track and field athlete ever, but she made it clear that her identity wasn't in her medals—it was in her faith. She often shares scripture and encouragement with her fans, reminding them to keep trusting God no matter what life throws at them. Through her athletic success, advocacy, and devotion to Christ, Allyson Felix shows the strength and steadfastness that comes from living out your faith every step of the way.

Felix's story encourages us to remain grounded in our faith, reminding us that steadfastness and faithfulness reach beyond immediate outcomes to influence lives and leave a legacy of hope and trust in God's promises.

STUDY PASSAGE

1 *²¹ And you, who once were alienated and hostile in mind, doing evil deeds, ²² he has now reconciled in his body of flesh by his death, in order to present you holy and blameless and above reproach before him, ²³ if indeed you continue in the faith, stable and steadfast, not shifting from the hope of the gospel that you heard, which has been proclaimed in all creation under heaven, and of which I, Paul, became a minister. (ESV)*

STUDY HELP

- *"alienated"*—This word emphasizes the separation between humanity and God due to sin. Studying "alienated" helps you see the significant impact of sin on your relationship with God and the need for reconciliation.

- *"reconciled"*—"Reconciled" points to the restoration of the relationship between God and humanity through Christ's sacrifice. This word is central to understanding the gospel and the work Christ accomplished on the cross.

- *"holy"*—"Holy" describes the transformed state believers are called to through Christ. It emphasizes that, in reconciliation, God doesn't merely forgive but sanctifies, setting believers apart as righteous and without blemish.

STUDY QUESTIONS

1. What does it mean to be "alienated" from God, and how does this concept help us understand the impact of sin on our relationship with Him?

_____

_____

_____

_____

2. How does Paul's description of us as "enemies in your minds because of your evil behavior" emphasize the need for internal as well as external transformation?

_____

_____

_____

_____

3. What does it mean that we have been "reconciled" to God by Christ's physical body through death, and why is this sacrifice essential for restoring our relationship with God?

_____

_____

_____

_____

4. How does being presented "holy, without blemish and free from accusation" impact your view of yourself and your relationship with God?

_____

_____

_____

_____

5. In verse 23, Paul stresses the importance of continuing in the faith, established and firm. Why is ongoing commitment to the faith essential, even after reconciliation with God?

_____

_____

_____

6. What practical steps can you take to "not move from the hope held out in the gospel" as Paul encourages in verse 23?

_____

_____

_____

_____

STUDY SUMMARY

Colossians 1:21-23 highlights the transformation believers experience through Christ: though once alienated from God and hostile in mind, they are now reconciled through Jesus' death to be presented holy and blameless before Him. This passage emphasizes the importance of continuing in faith, grounded in the hope of the gospel.

ATHLETE CONNECTION

The complete athlete emphasizes the importance of recognizing the transformative power of Christ's reconciliation, moving from alienation to a holy and blameless life, and strives to remain steadfast in that truth no matter what else is going on.

KEYS TO WINNING

▶ **VIDEO GUIDE AT KINGDOMSPORTS.ONLINE**

▶ TRANSFORMATION THROUGH RECONCILIATION

This passage reminds us that, though we were once alienated from God and hostile in mind, Christ's sacrifice has reconciled us to God. This transformative reconciliation changes our identity and restores our relationship with God, allowing us to live in peace with Him.

1. How does understanding that Christ's sacrifice has moved you from a place of alienation to reconciliation with God impact how you see yourself and your relationship with Him?

_____

_____

_____

_____

2. In what ways can you allow the peace that comes from reconciliation with God to shape your actions, relationships, and responses to challenges?

_____

_____

_____

_____

▶ THE NEW IDENTITY IN CHRIST

Through Christ's death, believers are presented as "holy, without blemish, and free from accusation" before God. This new identity encourages us to view ourselves through the lens of God's grace, recognizing that we are seen as pure and beloved in His eyes.

1. How does knowing that you are viewed by God as "holy, without blemish, and free from accusation" change the way you see yourself and approach your daily life? In what areas of your life could this truth bring greater freedom or peace?

_____

_____

_____

_____

2. In what ways can viewing yourself through the lens of God's grace help you extend that same grace to others?

_____

_____

_____

_____

▶ THE CALL TO PERSEVERE IN FAITH

Paul urges believers to continue in the faith, grounded and steadfast, highlighting the importance of perseverance. This takeaway emphasizes that while reconciliation is a gift, maintaining a close relationship with God requires an ongoing commitment to the hope of the gospel.

1. What does it mean to be "grounded and steadfast" in your faith, and how can you actively cultivate this perseverance in your daily life?

_____

_____

_____

_____

2. How does viewing reconciliation as a gift and a call to perseverance shape your approach to your relationship with God?

_____

_____

_____

_____

GAME CHANGER

Colossians 1:21-23 reminds us that, before knowing Christ, we were "alienated" from God, separated by sin and hostile in mind. This alienation wasn't just about actions; it was a complete separation from God. Realizing the impact of sin on our relationship with God can be sobering. However, this passage highlights that through Jesus' sacrifice, God reconciled us to Himself, bridging that separation.

In Christ, we are not only forgiven but also given a new identity: "holy, without blemish, and free from accusation" before God. This reconciliation doesn't merely cover our past mistakes; it transforms how God views us—pure, beloved, and accepted. For many, embracing this new identity takes faith and intentional reflection, especially when we may still feel imperfect. But this truth calls us to view ourselves through the lens of God's grace, letting go of accusations or guilt that may weigh on us. Through Christ, we stand unblemished before God, enabling us to approach Him with confidence, assured of our place in His family.

While Christ's sacrifice is sufficient for our redemption and security, we are called to perseverance daily. This daily faith walk involves cultivating habits like prayer, Scripture reading, and fellowship. As we stay rooted in the truth of our reconciliation, we reflect God's love to others, ministering to them with the transformative power of the gospel that made peace with God possible.

ONE BIG THING

What is the most significant lesson for you to take with you from this chapter?

_____

_____

_____

_____

_____

_____

_____

_____

_____

_____

_____

_____

_____

_____

_____

IMPACT PRAYER

Lord, thank You for reconciling me to Yourself through Christ, transforming my identity from alienated to beloved, holy, and blameless. Help me to see myself through the lens of Your grace, letting go of guilt and resting in the assurance of Your love. Strengthen me to stay grounded and steadfast in faith, continually rooted in the hope of the gospel. May my life reflect Your love and grace. In Jesus' name, Amen.

NOTES:

★ ★ ★

CHAPTER FIVE
THE COMPLETE ATHLETE

LABORS FOR OTHERS' MATURITY

COLOSSIANS 1:24-29

STUDY STARTER

Reggie White, known as the "Minister of Defense," wasn't just a Hall of Fame NFL defensive lineman—he was a man on a mission to help others grow in their faith. During his 15-year football career, White was a force on the field and a passionate advocate for Christ. As an ordained minister, since he was 17, he saw football as more than just a game—it was his platform to share the gospel. Whether leading Bible studies, hosting prayer meetings, or having personal conversations about faith, White was all about helping those around him mature spiritually. For him, winning games was great, but helping others grow in their relationship with Christ was the real goal.

White's ministry didn't stop at the locker room. He was deeply involved in his community, often spending time in underserved neighborhoods. He visited prisons, shelters, and schools, sharing the message that God's grace was for everyone—no matter their story. His down-to-earth, authentic approach made people feel seen and valued, inspiring many to take their faith more seriously or even start their journey with Christ. White believed that serving others was the best way to live out the gospel, and he prioritized lifting others up on and off the field.

Even after his football days were over, White stayed focused on helping others grow. He spoke at churches and conferences, mentored younger athletes, and encouraged them to use their platforms to glorify God. He constantly challenged believers to live out their faith in real, impactful ways, making sure his influence was about more than just football. Reggie White's life was all about servant leadership—putting others' spiritual maturity above his own comfort or fame. His legacy is a powerful reminder of what it means to labor for others to know Christ and experience His transformative power, leaving an eternal impact that goes way beyond the game.

In Colossians 1:24-29, Paul speaks of joyfully laboring and even suffering so that others might grow in maturity. White exemplifies a commitment to servant leadership, working tirelessly to uplift and support those in his care. White's example encourages us to labor with purpose, aiming to build others up in ways that honor God and lead to lasting impact.

STUDY PASSAGE

1 ²⁴ Now I rejoice in my sufferings for your sake, and in my flesh I am filling up what is lacking in Christ's afflictions for the sake of his body, that is, the church, ²⁵ of which I became a minister according to the stewardship from God that was given to me for you, to make the word of God fully known, ²⁶ the mystery hidden for ages and generations but now revealed to his saints. ²⁷ To them God chose to make known how great among the Gentiles are the riches of the glory of this mystery, which is Christ in you, the hope of glory. ²⁸ Him we proclaim, warning everyone and teaching everyone with all wisdom, that we may present everyone mature in Christ. ²⁹ For this I toil, struggling with all his energy that he powerfully works within me. (ESV)

STUDY HELP

- *"sufferings*—Paul's willingness to endure suffering for the sake of the church highlights the cost of discipleship and ministry.

- *"mystery*—"Mystery" refers to the previously hidden truth of the gospel that has now been revealed through Christ. This term demonstrates the nature of the unfolding plan of God and the significance of Christ's work being made known.

- *"maturity"*—Paul's goal in ministry is to present believers as mature in Christ, highlighting spiritual growth as a central focus of the Christian journey. Maturity means more than just knowledge; it's about living out what we know with wisdom, love, and steadfastness, showing Christ's qualities in our words, actions, and attitudes. Spiritual maturity involves continual growth toward being "complete" or "fully developed" in Christ.

STUDY QUESTIONS

1. What does Paul mean when he says he "rejoices in what I am suffering for you" (verse 24), and how can suffering be a source of joy in the context of ministry and serving others?

_____

_____

_____

_____

2. Paul mentions the "mystery" that was hidden for ages but is now revealed (verse 26). What is this mystery, and why is it significant to Paul's ministry? Consider the meaning of "mystery" in relation to God's redemptive plan through Christ.

_____

_____

_____

_____

3. How does the phrase "Christ in you, the hope of glory" (verse 27) shape your view of your relationship with Christ and your future hope as a believer?

_____

_____

_____

_____

4. Paul's goal is to "present everyone fully mature in Christ" (verse 28). What does maturity in Christ look like, and how can you pursue this maturity in your own life?

_____

_____

_____

_____

5. In verse 29, Paul says he "strenuously contends" with all the energy Christ provides. What does this teach about the balance between personal effort and reliance on God's strength in ministry and spiritual growth?

_____

_____

_____

_____

6. How does Paul's dedication to making known the gospel and maturing others in Christ challenge or encourage you in your own approach to discipleship and sharing your faith?

_____

_____

_____

_____

STUDY SUMMARY

Colossians 1:24-29 reveals Paul's dedication to his ministry, emphasizing his willingness to endure suffering to help believers grow into full maturity in Christ. He speaks of the mystery of "Christ in you, the hope of glory," highlighting his goal to proclaim Christ and present every believer as spiritually complete through God's strength working in him.

ATHLETE CONNECTION

The complete athlete embodies dedication, perseverance, and a commitment to fostering spiritual maturity in others. Just as Paul endures challenges to guide believers toward fullness in Christ, a believer is called to lead and inspire with patience, viewing every interaction as an opportunity to cultivate Christlike character in those they encounter.

KEYS TO WINNING

▶ **VIDEO GUIDE AT KINGDOMSPORTS.ONLINE**

▶ JOY IN SACRIFICIAL SERVICE

Paul rejoices in his sufferings for the sake of the church, showing that true ministry often involves personal sacrifice. This perspective encourages us to embrace challenges and sacrifices as part of serving others and advancing God's kingdom, finding joy in the impact our efforts have on others' spiritual growth.

1. How does Paul's example of rejoicing in suffering challenge your perspective on personal sacrifices and hardships you may face while serving others? Reflect on areas where you encounter difficulty or resistance in serving?

_____

_____

_____

_____

2. How can you find joy in the impact your efforts have on others' spiritual growth, even when it involves personal sacrifice or inconvenience?

_____

_____

_____

_____

▶ THE MYSTERY OF "CHRIST IN YOU"

Paul speaks of the mystery revealed in the gospel: "Christ in you, the hope of glory." This profound truth reminds us that the indwelling presence of Christ brings us hope, strength, and the assurance of God's promises, empowering us to live transformed lives that reflect His glory.

1. How does the reality of "Christ in you, the hope of glory" influence the way you view your own identity and purpose?

_____

_____

_____

_____

2. In what areas of your life do you need to rely more on the strength and hope that Christ's indwelling presence provides?

_____

_____

_____

_____

▸ COMMITMENT TO SPIRITUAL MATURITY

Paul's goal is to present every believer fully mature in Christ, highlighting the importance of discipleship and growth. This takeaway challenges us to actively pursue spiritual maturity in ourselves and to help others grow in their faith, relying on God's power to guide and sustain us in this mission.

1. In what ways are you actively pursuing spiritual maturity in your own life, and what steps can you take to grow further in your faith?

_____

_____

_____

_____

2. How can you encourage and support others in their journey toward spiritual maturity, and what role does discipleship play in this commitment? How can you help others grow in their faith while relying on God's strength and wisdom?

_____

_____

_____

_____

GAME CHANGER

Colossians 1:24-29 reveals Paul's profound commitment to his ministry, even to the point of rejoicing in his sufferings for the sake of the church. Paul sees his hardships as part of God's plan to bring others to faith and growth, and he endures them willingly to help others grow spiritually. This selfless dedication calls us to reflect on our own service and to embrace sacrifice as a necessary part of serving God and others. By viewing challenges as opportunities to help others know Christ, we can find joy in the purpose our efforts bring, even when the path is difficult.

In this passage, Paul also speaks of the "mystery" revealed through the gospel: "Christ in you, the hope of glory." This truth transforms the Christian journey from mere belief to a personal, empowering relationship with Jesus. Knowing that Christ dwells within us gives us hope, strength, and purpose beyond what we could achieve on our own. It's a reminder that we are not left to grow spiritually through our own efforts but are strengthened by the presence of Christ within. Through this mystery, we find assurance that His power is at work in us, empowering us to live in ways that reflect His character.

Ultimately, Paul's goal is to "present everyone fully mature in Christ," highlighting the importance of spiritual growth and discipleship. This commitment to maturity challenges us to pursue growth actively, relying on God's power to guide and sustain us. It encourages us to invest in the spiritual growth of others, just as Paul did, by helping them to grow in knowledge, faith, and character.

ONE BIG THING

What is the most significant lesson for you to take with you from this chapter?

_____

_____

_____

_____

_____

_____

_____

_____

_____

_____

_____

_____

_____

_____

_____

_____

IMPACT PRAYER

Lord, thank You for the example of Paul's dedication in serving You, even through suffering, for the sake of others' faith and growth. Help me to embrace challenges as opportunities to share Your love and truth, finding joy in the purpose You give my efforts. Thank You for the mystery of "Christ in me, the hope of glory," and may You strengthen me in my commitment to grow and help others to mature in their walk with You, relying always on Your power to guide and sustain me. In Jesus' name, Amen.

NOTES:

★ ★ ★

CHAPTER SIX
THE COMPLETE ATHLETE

PURSUES MATURE KNOWLEDGE

COLOSSIANS 2:1-7

STUDY STARTER

A.C. Green, the NBA Ironman known for his record-breaking 1,192 consecutive games, wasn't just focused on basketball—he was laser-focused on growing in his faith and pursuing a deeper knowledge of Christ. Throughout his career, Green made it clear that his priorities went far beyond the court. While many athletes concentrated on their stats and performance, Green poured his energy into spiritual growth, spending time studying the Bible and figuring out how to live out its teachings in his daily life. His relationship with Christ shaped everything—his values, his decisions, and how he treated others. He was all about maturing in his faith and helping others do the same.

Green's commitment to knowing Christ on a deeper level really stood out in how he handled the challenges of the NBA lifestyle. With all the fame, money, and temptations that come with being a pro athlete, it's easy to get sidetracked—but not Green. He leaned on prayer, fellowship, and daily time in God's Word to stay grounded. He also surrounded himself with mentors and Christian friends who kept him accountable and encouraged him to grow spiritually. Green didn't keep his faith to himself, either—he shared biblical truths with teammates, using his platform to help others understand Christ better.

After retiring, Green kept that same focus on growing in his faith and encouraging others to do the same. He started the A.C. Green Youth Foundation, which teaches young people about character, integrity, and faith. Through the foundation and his speaking engagements, Green inspires others to dig deeper into God's Word and make spiritual growth a priority. He always reminds people that pursuing maturity in Christ is a lifelong journey—it takes discipline, humility, and a hunger to know God better. A.C. Green's life shows that even in the spotlight, you can prioritize your spiritual development and inspire others to grow in theirs.

Just as Green exemplifies how athletes can prioritize their spiritual development and inspire others to do the same, Paul urges believers to deepen their knowledge of God's Word, allowing it to guide them with wisdom and confidence. When we are "rooted and built up" in Christ, in whom all the treasures of wisdom and knowledge are hidden, we are equipped to face challenges, make wise decisions, and stay steadfast in our convictions.

STUDY PASSAGE

2 *For I want you to know how great a struggle I have for you and for those at Laodicea and for all who have not seen me face to face, ² that their hearts may be encouraged, being knit together in love, to reach all the riches of full assurance of understanding and the knowledge of God's mystery, which is Christ, ³ in whom are hidden all the treasures of wisdom and knowledge. ⁴ I say this in order that no one may delude you with plausible arguments. ⁵ For though I am absent in body, yet I am with you in spirit, rejoicing to see your good order and the firmness of your faith in Christ. ⁶ Therefore, as you received Christ Jesus the Lord, so walk in him, ⁷ rooted and built up in him and established in the faith, just as you were taught, abounding in thanksgiving. (ESV)*

STUDY HELP

- *"encouraged"*—This Greek word, often translated as "encouraged," can also mean "comforted" or "strengthened." It carries the sense of being called alongside to provide support, as a friend or advocate might. In this context, Paul's use suggests a desire for the Colossian believers to be spiritually fortified and comforted in their hearts, reflecting not only encouragement but also deep reassurance in their faith.

- *"united"*—Paul emphasizes unity as foundational for a healthy Christian community. Focusing on "united" highlights the role of love in binding believers together, creating a bond that reflects Christ's love and fosters spiritual growth.

- *"rooted"*—This term is an agricultural metaphor meaning to be deeply and securely planted. It implies permanence and stability, suggesting that believers are deeply anchored in Christ. This image helps readers see that spiritual growth depends on a firm foundation, with "roots" in Christ providing strength and resilience, much like a tree's roots stabilize it against winds and storms.

STUDY QUESTIONS

1. In verse 2, Paul says his goal is for believers to be "encouraged in heart." What does it mean to be encouraged in heart, and how can this encouragement strengthen our faith and resilience?

_____

_____

_____

_____

2. Paul speaks of being "united in love" in verse 2. How does unity in love contribute to a strong Christian community, and what role do you play in fostering this unity?

_____

_____

_____

_____

3. What is the "mystery of God" that Paul speaks of in verse 2, and why is it significant that this mystery has now been revealed in Christ?

_____

_____

_____

_____

4. In verse 3, Paul says that "all the treasures of wisdom and knowledge" are hidden in Christ. How does this affect your view of where to seek wisdom and guidance for life's challenges?

_____

_____

_____

_____

5. Paul encourages believers to be "rooted and built up in him" (verse 7). What does it mean to be rooted in Christ, and how does this foundation impact your spiritual growth and ability to withstand challenges?

_____

_____

_____

_____

6. In verse 7, Paul speaks of "overflowing with thankfulness." How does gratitude play a role in maintaining a strong faith, and how can you cultivate thankfulness in your life, especially during challenges?

_____

_____

_____

_____

STUDY SUMMARY

This passage emphasizes Paul's desire for believers to be encouraged, united in love, and rooted in Christ, where all wisdom and knowledge are found. He encourages them to remain steadfast in their faith, growing strong and overflowing with thankfulness as they build their lives on Christ.

ATHLETE CONNECTION

The complete athlete knows the importance of encouraging others, fostering unity, and grounding one's work in Christ as the ultimate source of wisdom.

KEYS TO WINNING

▶ VIDEO GUIDE AT KINGDOMSPORTS.ONLINE

▶ THE IMPORTANCE OF ENCOURAGEMENT AND UNITY

Paul stresses the need for believers to be encouraged in heart and united in love, showing that spiritual support and unity are vital for a strong Christian community. This takeaway reminds us that mutual encouragement and love help us grow together in faith.

1. How can you actively contribute to creating a culture of encouragement and unity within your community or group, and what specific steps can you take to support others in their faith journey?

_____

_____

_____

_____

2. In what ways has mutual encouragement and love from others strengthened your own faith, and how can you share that same support with others?

_____

_____

_____

_____

▶ CHRIST AS THE SOURCE OF ALL WISDOM AND KNOWLEDGE

Paul highlights that all the treasures of wisdom and knowledge are found in Christ, emphasizing the sufficiency of Christ for understanding life's greatest questions and challenges. This encourages believers to seek wisdom in Christ, who provides true insight and guidance.

1. In what areas of your life are you seeking wisdom or guidance, and how can you intentionally turn to Christ as your primary source of insight and understanding? Reflect on how you usually approach life's questions or challenges?

_____

_____

_____

_____

2. What does it mean for you to view Christ as sufficient for life's deepest questions, and how can this belief shape your priorities and pursuits?

_____

_____

_____

_____

▶ THE NEED TO BE ROOTED AND ESTABLISHED

Paul encourages believers to be rooted, built up, and steadfast in their faith, grounded in the foundation of Christ. This image of rootedness serves as a reminder to develop a strong, resilient faith that can withstand challenges and grow through gratitude.

1. How can you deepen your roots in Christ, building a foundation to help you withstand life's challenges?

_____

_____

_____

_____

2. How does gratitude play a role in helping you grow and stay established in your faith, even during difficult times?

_____

_____

_____

_____

GAME CHANGER

In Colossians 2:1-7, Paul expresses his desire for believers to be "encouraged in heart and united in love." This encouragement and unity are not just for comfort; they are foundational for spiritual strength and growth. In our lives, encouragement from others and a sense of belonging in a faith community help us navigate challenges with resilience. Being "united in love" also reminds us that, as believers, we are interconnected, strengthening and supporting one another in our journey with Christ. Reflecting this unity, we draw closer to God and to each other, becoming a visible example of His love.

Paul then points us to Christ as the source of "all the treasures of wisdom and knowledge." This truth offers clarity and stability in a world of competing voices, guiding us to seek true wisdom and answers in Christ alone. His wisdom is sufficient for life's biggest questions, giving us a foundation we can trust and rely on. This wisdom points us back to the gospel, as Christ's life and teachings reveal God's ultimate plan for redemption and transformation. By making Christ our source of wisdom, we align our lives with His purposes, allowing His insights to shape our decisions, thoughts, and actions.

Finally, Paul encourages believers to be "rooted and built up" in Christ, reminding us that a strong faith foundation is essential for growth and resilience. Just as a tree withstands storms when firmly rooted, we can remain steadfast in difficult times when our faith is grounded in Christ. This rootedness invites us to live with gratitude, recognizing that every day, we are built up in Him, equipped to face challenges and grow deeper in our faith. Rooted in Christ and overflowing with thankfulness, we become witnesses of the gospel, showing others the strength and hope in a life built on Him.

ONE BIG THING

What is the most significant lesson for you to take with you from this chapter?

_____

_____

_____

_____

_____

_____

_____

_____

_____

_____

_____

_____

_____

_____

IMPACT PRAYER

Heavenly Father, thank You for the gift of encouragement and unity in Your love, which strengthens us in faith. Help us to seek all wisdom and knowledge in Christ, grounding our lives in His truth and guidance. As we root ourselves in You, may our faith grow strong and resilient, enabling us to face challenges with gratitude and hope. Let our lives be a reflection of Your love and wisdom, pointing others to the strength and peace found in You. In Jesus' name, Amen.

NOTES:

★ ★ ★

CHAPTER SEVEN
THE COMPLETE ATHLETES
GUARDS AGAINST DECEPTION

COLOSSIANS 2:8-15

STUDY STARTER

Manny Pacquiao, the legendary boxer and world champion, has made it a priority to guard against deception in his faith journey. Known for his humility and charisma, Pacquiao underwent a life-changing transformation when he became a born-again Christian in 2012. Before that, he openly admitted to living a life filled with vices and distractions—things he later realized were deceptive traps pulling him away from God. Since then, Manny has committed to staying grounded in truth, relying on the Bible to guide him in discerning what's real and what's not.

As Pacquiao's faith grew, he didn't shy away from sharing his beliefs—even when it meant clashing with societal norms or facing criticism. In interviews, he often quoted scripture and discussed the importance of living according to God's Word. He also warned about how easy it is to get misled by fame, wealth, and superficial success, which can make people feel self-sufficient but leave them spiritually empty. Despite the backlash, Pacquiao stayed firm, showing that guarding against deception meant standing by his convictions, no matter what.

Beyond his personal walk with God, Pacquiao uses his influence to encourage others to stay alert and guard against deception, too. Whether as a politician, philanthropist, or public speaker, he often talks about the importance of integrity, faith, and truth in every part of life. Pacquiao encourages people to measure their beliefs and choices against scripture and to seek wisdom through prayer and studying God's Word. His life is a powerful example of staying anchored in truth, rejecting the false promises of the world, and standing strong in faith—even when the pressure is on.

Just as Pacquiao's life serves as an example of how one can guard against spiritual deception by staying anchored in God's truth, rejecting worldly influences, and standing firm in faith, even in the face of opposition, Paul urges the Colossians to remain rooted in Christ, resisting empty ideas that lack real substance. Pacquiao's life and teaching remind us that real success is built on a solid foundation, not fleeting trends or surface-level fixes. His legacy challenges us to focus on what's genuine and lasting and reminds us that true spiritual growth comes from grounding ourselves in the sufficiency of Christ.

STUDY PASSAGE

2 *⁸ See to it that no one takes you captive by philosophy and empty deceit, according to human tradition, according to the elemental spirits of the world, and not according to Christ. ⁹ For in him the whole fullness of deity dwells bodily, ¹⁰ and you have been filled in him, who is the head of all rule and authority. ¹¹ In him also you were circumcised with a circumcision made without hands, by putting off the body of the flesh, by the circumcision of Christ, ¹² having been buried with him in baptism, in which you were also raised with him through faith in the powerful working of God, who raised him from the dead. ¹³ And you, who were dead in your trespasses and the uncircumcision of your flesh, God made alive together with him, having forgiven us all our trespasses, ¹⁴ by canceling the record of debt that stood against us with its legal demands. This he set aside, nailing it to the cross. ¹⁵ He disarmed the rulers and authorities and put them to open shame, by triumphing over them in him. (ESV)*

STUDY HELP

- *"deception"*—This term refers to a misleading or deceptive quality, implying the allure of something false. In verse 8, Paul warns believers to be cautious of philosophies that are "hollow and deceptive," pointing to teachings that may appear attractive or wise but lack truth and substance. Paul specifically calls out human traditions and "elemental spiritual forces" (often referring to worldly or demonic influences) as sources of deception.

- *"circumcision"*—In the Old Testament, circumcision was a sign of the covenant between God and Israel, marking them as God's people. Here, Paul speaks of a spiritual circumcision—a cutting away of the sinful nature—that occurs through Christ. This spiritual circumcision signifies a new identity, setting believers apart from sin through their union with Christ.

- *"forgiven"*—This term means to "show grace" or "to forgive." Paul uses it to describe the complete forgiveness of sins given through Christ. This forgiveness isn't just transactional; it's a free gift based on God's grace, wiping out the "charge of our legal indebtedness" (verse 14). The word points to both release and pardon, symbolizing the removal of all barriers to reconciliation with God. This spiritual circumcision signifies a new identity, setting believers apart from sin through their union with Christ.

STUDY QUESTIONS

1. In verse 8, Paul warns, "See to it that no one takes you captive by philosophy and empty deceit." What does Paul mean by "empty deceit," and why is it important to guard against teachings that are "according to human tradition"? Consider current influences that may lead people away from Christ?

_____

_____

_____

_____

2. Paul writes in verse 9, "For in him the whole fullness of deity dwells bodily." How does knowing that Christ embodies the fullness of God influence your relationship with Him?

_____

_____

_____

_____

3. What does this spiritual circumcision represent, and how does it reflect the transformation that comes from being in Christ? Think about the difference between outward practices and inner spiritual change?

_____

_____

_____

_____

4. Paul says in verse 12 that we are "buried with him in baptism, in which you were also raised with him." How does this imagery of burial and resurrection illustrate the believer's new life in Christ?

_____

_____

_____

_____

5. In verse 14, Paul writes that Christ "canceled the record of debt that stood against us." What does it mean to have this record of debt canceled, and how does understanding this forgiveness affect your relationship with God?

_____

_____

_____

_____

6. Verse 15 describes Christ disarming "the rulers and authorities" and triumphing over them. How does Christ's victory over spiritual powers encourage you to rely on Him in your own struggles?

_____

_____

_____

_____

STUDY SUMMARY

Colossians 2:8-15 warns believers against being misled by deceptive philosophies and emphasizes that the fullness of God dwells in Christ, who has reconciled us through His death and resurrection. In Christ, believers are spiritually transformed, fully forgiven, and share in His victory over all spiritual powers

ATHLETE CONNECTION

The complete athlete seeks Christ and His Word for spiritual growth, avoiding influences that distract from the gospel. They rely on the fullness, forgiveness, and victory found in Christ, helping them to live their lives with integrity, empower others spiritually, and stand strong against challenges of this world.

KEYS TO WINNING

▶ **VIDEO GUIDE AT KINGDOMSPORTS.ONLINE**

▶ STAY ROOTED IN CHRIST'S TRUTH

Paul warns against being taken captive by "philosophy and empty deceit," reminding believers to hold firmly to Christ's teachings and avoid worldly influences that stray from the gospel. This calls us to keep our beliefs and practices anchored in Christ alone.

1. In what areas of your life do you feel the pull of "empty deceit" or worldly influences, and how can you intentionally anchor yourself in Christ's teachings to resist these distractions?

_____

_____

_____

_____

2. How can you deepen your understanding of Christ's teachings to strengthen your foundation and help you discern between gospel truth and deceptive influences?

_____

_____

_____

_____

▸ THE FULLNESS OF GOD DWELLS IN CHRIST

Paul emphasizes that "in him the whole fullness of deity dwells bodily," affirming Christ's divinity and sufficiency. This means that believers have everything they need spiritually in Christ, who embodies the complete nature and power of God.

1. How does knowing that "the whole fullness of deity dwells bodily" in Christ impact your understanding of His power and sufficiency in your life? Reflect on what it means for Christ to embody the complete nature of God.

_____

_____

_____

_____

2. In what areas are you tempted to seek fulfillment outside of Christ, and how can recognizing His complete sufficiency help you turn back to Him as your source?

_____

_____

_____

_____

▸ CHRIST'S VICTORY AND OUR FORGIVENESS

Through Christ's death and resurrection, He has canceled our debts and triumphed over "rulers and authorities," granting us both forgiveness and freedom. This assures believers of their complete forgiveness and victory over spiritual opposition, empowering them to live confidently in God's grace.

1. How does understanding that Christ has canceled your debts and granted you complete forgiveness change the way you approach God and live out your faith daily?

_____

_____

_____

_____

2. In what areas of life do you feel spiritual opposition, and how can Christ's victory over "rulers and authorities" encourage you to face these challenges with confidence? Consider how Christ's triumph empowers you against fears or obstacles?

_____

_____

_____

_____

GAME CHANGER

Colossians 2:8-15 reminds us of the power and sufficiency of Christ, warning us not to be "taken captive by philosophy and empty deceit," which stray from the truth of the gospel. In a world full of competing ideas and beliefs, this passage calls us to remain anchored in Christ's teachings, ensuring our lives are built on His truth rather than fleeting cultural ideas. Holding firmly to Christ grounds us and protects us from the distractions and deceptions of the world. Reflecting on this warning encourages us to evaluate our lives, making sure we seek wisdom, fulfillment, and purpose in Him alone.

The passage also reveals the depth of Christ's divinity, stating that "in him the whole fullness of deity dwells bodily." This incredible truth assures us that Jesus is fully God, embodying all of God's nature and power. Knowing that we have access to the fullness of God in Christ means that we lack nothing spiritually. His presence brings all the wisdom, strength, and guidance we need. This realization points us back to the gospel—Christ is not only our Savior but our constant source, fully capable of meeting our deepest needs and guiding us through every season of life.

Ultimately, Paul's words remind us of Christ's victory and our complete forgiveness through His death and resurrection. By canceling the record of our debt, Christ has freed us from guilt and shame, and by triumphing over "rulers and authorities," He has secured victory over spiritual forces. This truth allows us to walk confidently in God's grace, empowered to live with purpose and freedom. In Christ, we are not only forgiven but are equipped to face life's challenges with the assurance that His victory is our victory.

ONE BIG THING

What is the most significant lesson for you to take with you from this chapter?

_____

_____

_____

_____

_____

_____

_____

_____

_____

_____

_____

_____

_____

_____

_____

_____

_____

_____

IMPACT PRAYER

Heavenly Father, thank You for the fullness of life and truth we have in Christ. Help us to stay rooted in Your Word, discerning truth amidst all that distracts us, and to remember that in Christ, we have everything we need. Thank You for canceling our debts and securing victory over all forces that oppose us. May we live in the freedom and confidence Your forgiveness brings, empowered by Your grace, to walk boldly and gratefully each day. In Jesus' name, Amen.

★ ★ ★

CHAPTER EIGHT

THE COMPLETE ATHLETE

REJECTS SELF-MADE RELIGION

COLOSSIANS 2:16-23

STUDY STARTER

Clayton Kershaw, the star pitcher for the Los Angeles Dodgers and one of baseball's all-time greats, is a powerful example of someone who turned away from self-made religion to embrace a Christ-centered faith. Early in his career, Kershaw thought being good and following some basic moral rules was enough to define his faith. But as he navigated the pressures of professional sports and the temptations that come with fame, he realized his approach was shallow. Relying on his own efforts and surface-level religious habits left him without the deep relationship with Christ he truly needed.

Things began to change when Kershaw and his wife, Ellen, decided to make their faith a priority. They dug into Scripture, prayed more, and focused on serving others. Kershaw came to understand that real faith meant surrendering his life to Christ and living according to God's Word, not just following his own rules. Rejecting the idea of self-made religion, he embraced the gospel's message of grace and salvation through Jesus. This shift gave his faith real depth and reshaped how he saw his career and platform. Today, Kershaw openly credits God for his abilities and believes his purpose goes far beyond baseball.

You can see Kershaw's commitment to this new perspective in how he lives his life. Through Kershaw's Challenge, a charity he runs with Ellen, he works to serve underprivileged communities around the world. He also uses his platform to share the gospel, reminding others that faith isn't about checking religious boxes but having a real relationship with Christ. By letting go of self-reliance and trusting in God's grace, Clayton Kershaw shows how a Christ-centered faith can transform not only a life but also the lives of others through service and inspiration.

Kershaw's approach reflects Paul's message in Colossians 2:16-23, where Paul warns believers against relying on strict rules or "self-made religion" as a means of spirituality. Like Paul, who encourages believers to focus on their relationship with Christ rather than restrictive practices, Kershaw shows that self-made rules alone can't enforce unity and commitment.

STUDY PASSAGE

2 *¹⁶ Therefore let no one pass judgment on you in questions of food and drink, or with regard to a festival or a new moon or a Sabbath. ¹⁷ These are a shadow of the things to come, but the substance belongs to Christ. ¹⁸ Let no one disqualify you, insisting on asceticism and worship of angels, going on in detail about visions, puffed up without reason by his sensuous mind, ¹⁹ and not holding fast to the Head, from whom the whole body, nourished and knit together through its joints and ligaments, grows with a growth that is from God. ²⁰ If with Christ you died to the elemental spirits of the world, why, as if you were still alive in the world, do you submit to regulations—²¹ "Do not handle, Do not taste, Do not touch" ²² (referring to things that all perish as they are used)—according to human precepts and teachings? ²³ These have indeed an appearance of wisdom in promoting self-made religion and asceticism and severity to the body, but they are of no value in stopping the indulgence of the flesh. (ESV)*

STUDY HELP

- *"judgment"*—In verse 16, Paul warns believers not to let others judge them regarding practices like dietary rules, festivals, and Sabbaths. Paul's caution suggests that such judgments were being imposed by those who still emphasized adherence to Old Testament laws or additional human traditions as necessary for spiritual maturity.

- *"shadow"*—This term refers to a "shadow" or "outline," suggesting something incomplete or insubstantial compared to the actual reality. In verse 17, Paul uses it to describe religious rituals and practices as a shadow of the true substance found in Christ. These practices pointed to God's future redemptive work but were only a temporary foreshadowing of Christ's ultimate fulfillment.

- *"asceticism"*—Although commonly translated as "asceticism," the underlying Greek term literally means "humility" or "self-abasement." In this context, it likely refers to practices of extreme self-denial, which were promoted by some as necessary for spiritual enlightenment or purity. In verse 18, Paul warns against being disqualified by those insisting on asceticism, as these practices can distract from true faith and create a false sense of superiority.

STUDY QUESTIONS

1. In verse 16, Paul says, "let no one pass judgment on you in questions of food and drink, or with regard to a festival or a new moon or a Sabbath." Why does Paul caution against judgment based on these religious practices, and how can we apply this principle today?

_____

_____

_____

_____

2. Paul describes these practices as a "shadow of the things to come" in verse 17. What does it mean that they are a shadow, and how does focusing on Christ as the substance help us understand the gospel more fully?

_____

_____

_____

_____

3. In verse 18, Paul warns against those who promote "asceticism and worship of angels." What is asceticism, and how can practices that seem spiritual distract from a true relationship with Christ?

_____

_____

_____

_____

4. Paul speaks in verse 19 of holding fast to "the Head, from whom the whole body... grows with a growth that is from God." How does being connected to Christ as the Head influence your spiritual growth and unity within the Christian community?

_____

_____

_____

_____

5. In verse 20, Paul asks why believers "submit to regulations" if they have died with Christ to the "elemental spirits of the world." How does understanding your freedom in Christ influence your approach to religious rules or external expectations?

_____

_____

_____

_____

6. Verse 23 mentions that these regulations "have an appearance of wisdom...but they are of no value in stopping the indulgence of the flesh." How can focusing on Christ rather than external rules lead to true transformation?

_____

_____

_____

_____

STUDY SUMMARY

Colossians 2:16-23 warns believers not to be judged by or bound to religious rituals, emphasizing that these practices are merely shadows of the reality found in Christ. Paul encourages believers to hold fast to Christ, the source of true spiritual growth, and to reject human regulations that appear wise but lack the power to transform the heart.

ATHLETE CONNECTION

The complete athlete prioritizes authentic spiritual growth over rigid practices, helping others develop a faith rooted in the Word of God rather than in mere rituals or human expectations.

KEYS TO WINNING

▶ **VIDEO GUIDE AT KINGDOMSPORTS.ONLINE**

▶ FREEDOM FROM JUDGMENT BASED ON RITUALS

Paul encourages believers not to let others judge them regarding dietary laws, religious festivals, or the Sabbath, reminding us that Christ has freed us from being bound to these external practices. This takeaway highlights that true faith isn't about following specific rituals but about a personal, transformative relationship with Jesus through His revealed Word.

1. In what ways have you felt pressured to conform to certain practices or expectations in your faith, and how does recognizing your freedom in Christ help you focus on a more personal relationship with Him?

_____

_____

_____

_____

2. How can you prioritize a transformative relationship with Jesus over rituals or outward practices, and what changes might this bring to your daily walk with Him?

_____

_____

_____

_____

▶ CHRIST AS THE SUBSTANCE OVERSHADOWS

Religious rituals are described as a "shadow" of what's fulfilled in Christ, pointing to Him as the true reality. This encourages believers to focus on the substance—Christ Himself—rather than on practices that symbolically point to Him, deepening our understanding of faith centered in Christ.

1. In what areas of your life are you tempted to focus on outward practices or routines rather than deepening your relationship with Christ, the true substance of your faith?

_____

_____

_____

_____

2. How does viewing Christ as the fulfillment of all spiritual practices and symbols change how you understand and approach your faith?

_____

_____

_____

_____

▶ TRUTH MATURITY COMES FROM
HOLDING FAST TO CHRIST

Paul stresses that spiritual growth and strength come from being connected to Christ, the Head of the body. This teaches us that authentic transformation isn't found in external regulations but in a deep, reliant relationship with Christ, who provides the growth that is from God.

1. In what ways are you currently relying on external practices or personal efforts for spiritual growth, and how can you shift to a deeper dependence on Christ as the true source of maturity?

_____

_____

_____

_____

2. Consider what it means to grow by relying on Christ rather than on external rules. How can you prioritize this connection with Christ in your daily life to experience authentic growth, and how is it connected to knowing His Word?

_____

_____

_____

_____

GAME CHANGER

In this text, Paul addresses the pressures of religious judgment and ritual, encouraging believers not to let others "pass judgment" on them based on outward practices like dietary laws or religious festivals. This passage brings tremendous relief for those struggling to measure up to external expectations. Paul's message reminds us that our faith is not about strict adherence to rituals but our freedom in Christ. This freedom shifts our focus from gaining approval through practices to building a genuine relationship with

Jesus. Recognizing this truth helps us let go of comparison and judgment, finding rest in the acceptance that Christ has already given us.

Paul describes these religious observances as a "shadow" of things to come, with Christ being the true substance. This powerful metaphor illustrates that rituals were always meant to point us toward the fullness found in Jesus. When we focus on Christ as the center, our faith becomes more than a set of rules; it becomes a relationship grounded in Him and His Word. Christ fulfills every need that rituals only symbolized, giving us direct access to God through His sacrifice. This reminder points us back to the gospel, the good news that Christ alone is sufficient and that we have everything we need in Him for a vibrant, growing faith.

Ultimately, Paul urges believers to hold fast to Christ, who is the Head of the body and the source of true growth. Spiritual maturity comes not from following rules but from staying connected to Christ. His presence provides the strength and guidance that leads to authentic transformation. This passage calls us to pursue a deeper, more reliant relationship with Christ, trusting that He will shape and grow us from within. In Christ, we find the freedom, fulfillment, and growth we need—gifts that flow from His grace rather than our own efforts.

ONE BIG THING

What is the most significant lesson from this chapter for you to take with you?

_____

_____

_____

_____

_____

_____

_____

_____

IMPACT PRAYER

Lord, thank You for the freedom and fullness we have in Christ, who has freed us from the burden of trying to earn approval through rituals. Help us to center our lives on Him, the true substance of our faith, and let go of anything that distracts us from a genuine relationship with You. Teach us to hold fast to Christ each day, relying on His presence for real transformation and growth. May our lives reflect the beauty of the gospel, living not by rules but by the grace and strength that come from knowing Him. In Jesus' name, Amen.

★ ★ ★

CHAPTER NINE

THE COMPLETE ATHLETE

PUTS OFF THE OLD MAN

COLOSSIANS 3:1-11

STUDY STARTER

Darryl Strawberry, the former MLB star who played for the Mets and Yankees, is an incredible example of someone who left behind an old way of life to embrace a new one in Christ. During his baseball career, Strawberry was one of the most talented players of his time, but his life off the field was a mess. Addiction, legal troubles, and destructive choices consumed him as he chased fame, money, and fleeting pleasures. Despite all his success, his life was spiraling out of control, and it wasn't until he hit rock bottom multiple times that he finally surrendered to God.

Strawberry's turning point came when he encountered Christ and decided to leave his old life behind. Through faith, prayer, and guidance from mentors, he made the hard choice to "put off the old man"—letting go of the toxic habits and mindset that had defined him for years. He got clean, repaired broken relationships, and immersed himself in studying the Bible to renew his heart and mind. Strawberry often talks about how God's grace gave him the strength to overcome his past and step into a new life focused on purpose and obedience to Christ. He now sees himself as a "new creation," fully transformed by Jesus.

Today, Strawberry is a pastor, author, and speaker who spends his time helping others find the same hope and freedom he did. Through his ministry, he shares his story to show that no one is too far gone for God's redemption. He emphasizes the need to put off the old self every day, leaning on God's strength to keep growing and changing. His life is proof of how the gospel can bring real, lasting transformation, turning a life of brokenness into one of service, faith, and impact.

Paul urges believers in Colossians 3:1-1 to "put off" the old self and embrace their new life rooted in Christ. Just as Strawberry surrendered his defeatist mindset and adopted a culture of excellence, Paul calls believers to let go of worldly attitudes and behaviors that hinder their growth and success in their battle against sin. Lasting change begins when we put off the destructive ways of the world and set our minds on things above.

STUDY PASSAGE

3 *If then you have been raised with Christ, seek the things that are above, where Christ is, seated at the right hand of God. ² Set your minds on things that are above, not on things that are on earth. ³ For you have died, and your life is hidden with Christ in God. ⁴ When Christ who is your life appears, then you also will appear with him in glory.*

⁵ Put to death therefore what is earthly in you: sexual immorality, impurity, passion, evil desire, and covetousness, which is idolatry. ⁶ On account of these the wrath of God is coming. ⁷ In these you too once walked, when you were living in them. ⁸ But now you must put them all away: anger, wrath, malice, slander, and obscene talk from your mouth. ⁹ Do not lie to one another, seeing that you have put off the old self with its practices ¹⁰ and have put on the new self, which is being renewed in knowledge after the image of its creator. ¹¹ Here there is not Greek and Jew, circumcised and uncircumcised, barbarian, Scythian, slave, free; but Christ is all, and in all. (ESV)

STUDY HELP

- **"seek"** – In verse 1, Paul calls believers to "seek the things that are above," suggesting a purposeful pursuit of heavenly values and priorities. This verb indicates that seeking is more than a passive wish; it's an active, ongoing pursuit of God's will, reflecting a heart and mind set on spiritual things.

- **"put to death"** – The Greek term for "put to death," is a strong word that literally means "to make dead" or "to render powerless." In verse 5, Paul commands believers to "put to death" sinful behaviors and desires associated with earthly living. This language is intentional, portraying sin as something that must be decisively and permanently renounced.

- *"renewed"* – In verse 10, Paul describes the "new self" as "being renewed in knowledge after the image of its creator." This renewal is not a one-time event but a continuous spiritual transformation as believers grow in their understanding of and relationship with God. It implies a dynamic process where believers are progressively restored to reflect God's image.

STUDY QUESTIONS

1. In verse 1, Paul encourages believers to "seek the things that are above." What does it mean to actively seek heavenly things, and how can this pursuit shape your daily priorities?

_____

_____

_____

_____

2. Verse 2 says to "set your minds on things that are above, not on things that are on earth." How does adopting a heavenly mindset influence the way you view and respond to worldly matters?

_____

_____

_____

_____

3. Paul instructs believers in verse 5 to "put to death" earthly behaviors. What does it mean to put sin to death, and why is this a crucial step in the believer's life?

_____

_____

_____

_____

4. In verse 9, Paul calls believers to "put off the old self with its practices." What does the "old self" represent, and how can you identify and discard old habits that don't align with your identity in Christ?

_____

_____

_____

_____

5. Verse 10 speaks of the "new self, which is being renewed in knowledge after the image of its creator." How does growing in the knowledge of God contribute to your spiritual renewal and transformation?

_____

_____

_____

_____

6. In verse 11, Paul emphasizes unity in Christ, saying there is no "Greek and Jew, circumcised and uncircumcised" in the new self. How does this new identity in Christ promote unity?

_____

_____

_____

_____

STUDY SUMMARY

Colossians 3:1-11 calls believers to set their minds on heavenly things, shedding old sinful habits and embracing a new identity in Christ. Paul emphasizes transformation through spiritual renewal, urging believers to live in unity, reflecting the image of Christ in all they do.

ATHLETE CONNECTION

The complete athlete sets the example by focusing on Christ-centered values, discarding harmful, sinful habits, and embracing a renewed identity in Christ.

KEYS TO WINNING

▶ **VIDEO GUIDE AT KINGDOMSPORTS.ONLINE**

▶ FOCUS ON HEAVENLY PRIORITIES

Paul urges believers to "seek the things that are above" and "set your minds on things that are above," emphasizing the importance of focusing on God's values rather than earthly distractions. This encourages believers to prioritize a mindset and lifestyle that reflects their identity in Christ.

1. How can you incorporate regular confession and repentance into your life, and what impact do you believe this will have on your relationship with God and others?

_____

_____

_____

_____

2. Reflecting on the Israelites' public confession, how can you foster a culture of openness and accountability within your community or church to encourage repentance (James 5:16)?

_____

_____

_____

_____

▶ PUT OFF THE OLD SELF

Paul calls for believers to "put to death" earthly, sinful behaviors, showing that true transformation involves decisively rejecting past habits and actions that conflict with a life in Christ. This takeaway highlights the importance of actively resisting sin as part of spiritual growth.

1. What old habits or behaviors in your life conflict with your new identity in Christ, and how can you take intentional steps to "put them to death" with God's help?

_____

_____

_____

2. How does viewing transformation as an ongoing process of actively rejecting sin change your approach to spiritual growth?

_____

_____

_____

▶ EMBRACE UNITY AND RENEWAL IN CHRIST

In the "new self," there is no division, and believers are "being renewed in knowledge after the image of its creator." This emphasizes that the new identity in Christ promotes unity across differences and invites ongoing spiritual renewal, encouraging believers to reflect God's image together.

1. How can you actively contribute to unity within your church, setting aside differences to reflect the new identity you share in Christ?

_____

_____

_____

_____

2. How does understanding renewal as an ongoing process inspire you to seek growth and knowledge in your relationship with God daily?

_____

_____

_____

_____

GAME CHANGER

Colossians 3:1-11 calls believers to a new way of life, rooted in Christ and focused on heavenly priorities. Paul urges us to "seek the things that are above" and to set our minds on what is eternal, not on earthly distractions. This shift in focus challenges us to reevaluate our goals, desires, and daily choices, prioritizing God's values over worldly pursuits. Keeping our thoughts and hearts aligned with Christ reminds us that our true identity and purpose are found in Him. This call to seek the things above isn't just about an occasional thought—it's about a consistent, intentional pursuit of Christ that reshapes our lives.

Paul emphasizes the importance of "putting to death" the old self, which includes earthly behaviors and attitudes that hinder our growth in Christ. The gospel invites us into true transformation, but it also requires us to consciously choose to reject patterns of sin. As we grow in our faith, we're called to let go of habits, mindsets, and reactions that don't reflect the character of Christ. This is a powerful reminder that spiritual growth is active; it's about taking steps to resist sin daily, leaning on God's strength to make real changes in our lives.

Finally, Colossians 3:1-11 reminds us that, in Christ, we are part of a unified and continually renewing body of believers. In this new identity, divisions fade, and we are being renewed "in knowledge after the image of its creator." This means that our journey in Christ is one of continuous growth, shaped by His truth and empowered by His grace. Through this renewal, we become more like Christ, reflecting His love and unity with others. This passage points us back to the gospel's transformative power, calling us to live out our faith with purpose, allowing Christ's presence within us to shine for others.

ONE BIG THING

What is the most significant lesson for you to take with you from this chapter?

_____
_____
_____
_____
_____
_____
_____
_____
_____
_____

IMPACT PRAYER

Lord, thank You for our new life in Christ and the invitation to seek what is above, focusing our hearts on You. Help us to let go of old patterns that keep us from growing, giving us the strength to put to death anything that hinders our walk with You. Renew us daily in Your image, filling us with a spirit of unity and purpose so we may reflect Your love and grace in all we do. In Jesus' name, Amen.

NOTES:

★ ★ ★

CHAPTER TEN
THE COMPLETE ATHLETE
PUTS ON THE NEW MAN

COLOSSIANS 3:12-16

STUDY STARTER

Montell Owens, a former NFL fullback and two-time Pro Bowl player strives to continually "put on the new man." During his career with the Jacksonville Jaguars and later teams, Owens was known for his work ethic and leadership and his strong faith, which transformed how he lived and played.

Early in his career, Owens, like many professional athletes, focused heavily on personal success and performance. However, as he matured, he realized that his life was about more than football and achievements. Owens decided to fully commit his life to Christ, recognizing that his identity wasn't in his career but in his faith. He embraced the call to "put on the new man" by living with compassion, humility, kindness, and a Christ-centered focus.

This transformation was evident in how Owens interacted with teammates, coaches, and fans. Known for his humility and selflessness, he prioritized the needs of the team over personal glory and was quick to mentor younger players, offering encouragement and spiritual support. He regularly participated in team Bible studies and prayer groups, using his platform to share his testimony and point others toward Christ. Owens also worked to stay grounded in God's Word, allowing it to shape his decisions and actions both on and off the field.

After retiring from football, Owens continued to live out his faith by serving his community and inspiring others. He often speaks about how his relationship with Christ gave him purpose beyond the game and how putting on the new man is a daily commitment to live in alignment with God's will. Through his life and testimony, Owens demonstrates that true success comes not from personal achievements but from a life rooted in Christ and dedicated to serving others. His journey is a powerful example of how faith can transform a career and a legacy.

Owen's life change mirrors Paul's instruction in Colossians 3:12-16, where believers are called to "put off" negative behaviors and actively "put on" virtues like compassion, kindness, humility, and patience. Paul recognizes that transformation requires more than just shedding sinful attitudes and habits; it calls for replacing them with Christ-like qualities.

STUDY PASSAGE

3 *¹² Put on then, as God's chosen ones, holy and beloved, compassionate hearts, kindness, humility, meekness, and patience, ¹³ bearing with one another and, if one has a complaint against another, forgiving each other; as the Lord has forgiven you, so you also must forgive. ¹⁴ And above all these put on love, which binds everything together in perfect harmony. ¹⁵ And let the peace of Christ rule in your hearts, to which indeed you were called in one body. And be thankful. ¹⁶ Let the word of Christ dwell in you richly, teaching and admonishing one another in all wisdom, singing psalms and hymns and spiritual songs, with thankfulness in your hearts to God. (ESV)*

STUDY HELP

- *"compassionate hearts"*—This word suggests a deep, heartfelt empathy that moves one to care for others with sensitivity and kindness. It implies a readiness to be emotionally invested in the lives of others, particularly in their suffering, and is often associated with God's merciful nature. In the cultural context, compassion reflects the care that God shows toward humanity, calling believers to imitate His kindness.

- *"love"*—This is the Greek word for selfless, sacrificial love, which seeks the highest good of others without expecting anything in return. In verse 14, Paul calls love the binding force that holds all virtues together "in perfect harmony." This suggests that love is foundational—it integrates other virtues and creates a unity that cannot be achieved through mere obligation. Love here is active and transformational, reflecting God's unconditional love toward us.

- *"thankful"*—This word implies an attitude of gratitude rooted in an awareness of God's grace and blessings. In the context of verse 15, Paul's command to "be thankful" reflects an inner posture that acknowledges God's goodness regardless of circumstances, encouraging believers to cultivate joy and peace by focusing on God's work in their lives.

STUDY QUESTIONS

1. In verse 12, Paul urges believers to "put on" qualities like compassion, kindness, humility, meekness, and patience. What does it mean to "put on" these virtues, and how can you practice embodying them in your daily life?

_____

_____

_____

_____

2. Verse 13 calls us to forgive others as the Lord has forgiven us. How does understanding Christ's forgiveness toward you shape the way you approach forgiveness in your own life?

_____

_____

_____

_____

3. Paul says in verse 14, "above all these put on love." Why does Paul place such a high priority on love, and how does love bind all other virtues together in harmony?

_____

_____

_____

_____

4. In verse 15, Paul encourages believers to "let the peace of Christ rule in your hearts." What does it mean for Christ's peace to "rule" in your heart, and how can you cultivate this peace amid daily challenges?

_____

_____

_____

_____

5. Paul emphasizes thankfulness in verse 15, saying, "And be thankful." How does a spirit of gratitude impact your outlook on life and your interactions with others?

_____

_____

_____

_____

6. Verse 16 calls believers to "let the word of Christ dwell in you richly." How can immersing yourself in God's Word influence your spiritual growth and the way you teach and encourage others?

_____

_____

_____

_____

STUDY SUMMARY

Colossians 3:12-16 calls believers to embody Christlike virtues—compassion, kindness, humility, forgiveness, and love—while allowing the peace of Christ and gratitude to guide their hearts. Paul emphasizes the importance of letting God's Word dwell richly within, shaping our interactions and building a unified, spiritually grounded community.

ATHLETE CONNECTION

The complete athlete strive to live with Christlike qualities such as compassion, patience, and love, fostering a spirit of unity and gratitude, and understands the importance of not only share with others what not to do but that it is just as important to show them what they should be doing.

KEYS TO WINNING

▶ VIDEO GUIDE AT KINGDOMSPORTS.ONLINE

▶ EMBRACE CHRISTLIKE VIRTUES

Paul calls believers to "put on" qualities like compassion, kindness, humility, meekness, and patience, reflecting Christ's character. This emphasizes the importance of actively embodying these virtues in our relationships, helping to build a loving and supportive community.

1. Which virtues—compassion, kindness, humility, meekness, or patience—do you find most challenging to embody, and what steps can you take to actively grow in this area?

_____

_____

_____

_____

2. How does intentionally "putting on" these virtues change how you interact with others, especially in difficult situations? How does it contrast to "putting off," and why is it important to do both?

_____

_____

_____

_____

▶ PRIORITIZE LOVE AND FORGIVENESS

Paul highlights love as the virtue that binds all others in harmony and calls believers to forgive as Christ forgave them. This shows that love and forgiveness are foundational for unity and peace within the body of Christ and foster healthy, grace-filled relationships.

1. How can you practice a deeper, Christlike love that brings unity to your relationships, especially in moments of tension or disagreement?

_____

_____

_____

_____

2. How does reflecting on Christ's forgiveness toward you impact your willingness to forgive others, even when it's difficult?

_____

_____

_____

_____

▶ CULTIVATE GRATITUDE AND THE PEACE OF CHRIST

By encouraging gratitude and allowing the peace of Christ to rule in our hearts, Paul shows how these attitudes shape our mindset and interactions. Living with thankfulness and inner peace helps believers remain grounded in their faith, even amidst challenges.

1. How can you make gratitude a daily practice that influences your perspective, even during difficult times?

_____

_____

_____

_____

2. What steps can you take to let the peace of Christ "rule in your heart," especially when facing stress or conflict?

_____

_____

_____

_____

GAME CHANGER

Colossians 3:12-16 calls us to embody qualities that reflect Christ—compassion, kindness, humility, meekness, and patience—not only as virtues to avoid the negative but as positive attributes we actively pursue. Paul describes these virtues as garments to "put on" as God's chosen people, holy and beloved. This imagery invites us to purposefully clothe ourselves with these qualities, treating others with grace even in challenging situations. These virtues become more than occasional responses; they reflect a continual transformation rooted in our identity in Christ. When we choose to act with compassion and kindness, we show others a tangible expression of God's love and model what it means to be truly valued and cared for.

The passage further underscores the importance of love and forgiveness, describing love as the unifying virtue that binds all others in harmony. Paul's instruction to "forgive as the Lord forgave you" serves as a reminder of the grace extended to us through Christ's sacrifice. This grace releases us from condemnation and calls us to restore relationships with others. Forgiveness becomes an act of imitating Christ, breaking cycles of bitterness, and fostering healing. By embracing both love and forgiveness, we cultivate a community where grace flows freely, encouraging reconciliation and unity.

Paul also urges us to "let the peace of Christ rule in your hearts" and to embrace a spirit of thankfulness. This peace, grounded in our security in Christ, enables us to face life's challenges with calm assurance. Likewise, gratitude helps us recognize God's ongoing goodness, anchoring us in His faithfulness. By letting Christ's peace guide us and practicing gratitude, we become testimonies of the gospel's transformative power, radiating joy and stability that draw others to God's love. Through these virtues, we don't just avoid negative behaviors; we positively the qualities of Christlikeness, pointing others to the hope and love found in Him.

ONE BIG THING

What is the most significant lesson for you to take with you from this chapter?

_____

_____

_____

_____

_____

_____

_____

_____

_____

_____

_____

_____

_____

_____

_____

_____

IMPACT PRAYER

Heavenly Father, grant us the grace to put on these virtues each day, forgiving others as You have forgiven us and letting Your peace rule in our hearts. Teach us to live in gratitude, seeing Your blessings in every circumstance, and to create harmony in our relationships through Your love. May our lives be a testimony of the life-changing grace. In Jesus' name, Amen.

NOTES:

★ ★ ★

CHAPTER ELEVEN

THE COMPLETE ATHLETE

SERVES CHRIST IN EVERYTHING

COLOSSIANS 3:17-4:1

STUDY STARTER

Stephen Curry, the NBA superstar and Golden State Warriors point guard, is a great example of someone who strives to serve Christ in everything he does. From the beginning of his career, Curry has been open about his faith, always pointing to God as the source of his talent and success. He's known for his humility, and you'll often see "I can do all things" written on his basketball shoes—a nod to Philippians 4:13. For Curry, this isn't just a cool slogan; it's a personal reminder that his gifts and accomplishments are meant to glorify God, not himself. Whether hitting a game-winning shot or facing adversity, he uses every moment to show that his identity is grounded in Christ, not just basketball.

Curry's faith goes beyond the court—it's woven into every part of his life. He's deeply involved in charitable work, like partnering with Nothing But Nets to help fight malaria in Africa. He also started Unanimous Media, a production company that creates family-friendly content with faith-based values. Whether working on community projects, speaking in interviews, or leading philanthropic efforts, Curry sees it all as an opportunity to honor Christ and make a meaningful impact. He doesn't separate his faith from his career or public life; it's all connected for him.

Off the court, Curry's commitment to Christ shines in how he approaches his roles as a husband, father, and follower of Jesus. He often talks about how his faith keeps him grounded and helps him balance the demands of fame, family, and his career. His example encourages fans and fellow athletes alike to live with purpose, humility, and a focus on what truly matters.

In Colossians 3, Paul encourages believers to do everything, "whether in word or deed," in the name of the Lord, treating others with love, respect, and humility. Paul urges Christians to serve wholeheartedly, finding true success not in personal gain but in lifting one another up. This principle reminds us that serving one another in any community—a church, a family, or a team—creates a foundation of unity and purpose and honors God.

STUDY PASSAGE

3 [17] *And whatever you do, in word or deed, do everything in the name of the Lord Jesus, giving thanks to God the Father through him.* [18] *Wives, submit to your husbands, as is fitting in the Lord.* [19] *Husbands, love your wives, and do not be harsh with them.* [20] *Children, obey your parents in everything, for this pleases the Lord.* [21] *Fathers, do not provoke your children, lest they become discouraged.* [22] *Bondservants, obey in everything those who are your earthly masters, not by way of eye-service, as people-pleasers, but with sincerity of heart, fearing the Lord.* [23] *Whatever you do, work heartily, as for the Lord and not for men,* [24] *knowing that from the Lord you will receive the inheritance as your reward. You are serving the Lord Christ.* [25] *For the wrongdoer will be paid back for the wrong he has done, and there is no partiality.*

4 *Masters, treat your bondservants justly and fairly, knowing that you also have a Master in heaven. (ESV)*

STUDY HELP

- *"word and deed"*—In verse 17, Paul includes "word" alongside "deed" to show that everything a believer says should align with the character of Christ. Logos in this context emphasizes the power and responsibility of our speech, reminding believers that their words reflect their faith and commitment to Jesus.

- *"household code"*—The "household code" in Colossians 3:18-4:1 is a set of instructions Paul provides for the Christian household, covering relationships between husbands and wives, parents and children, and masters and servants. This code outlines specific behaviors and attitudes that promote harmony, respect, and Christ-centered living within the family and household structure. Rather than reflecting the authoritarian structures typical of the Greco-Roman culture, Paul's instructions are rooted in mutual respect and responsibility, with each role guided by a commitment to Christ and His teachings.

- *"work heartily"*—This phrase indicates that believers should approach their work with full dedication, not just performing tasks for human approval but as an act of worship for God. This understanding elevates all forms of work—whether mundane or significant—to an offering for God, done with sincerity, integrity, and purpose.

STUDY QUESTIONS

1. In Colossians 3:17, Paul says to do everything "in the name of the Lord Jesus." What does it mean to live in a way that represents Jesus in both "word and deed," and how can this influence your everyday actions?

_____

_____

_____

_____

2. In verse 18, Paul instructs wives to submit to their husbands "as is fitting in the Lord." What does submission mean within marriage?

_____

_____

_____

_____

3. Verse 19 calls on husbands to love their wives and "not be harsh with them." What does it teach about the Christlike approach to leadership roles?

_____

_____

_____

_____

4. In verse 20, Paul encourages children to obey their parents "in everything." Why is obedience important in the family context, and how does it contribute to a respectful and harmonious household?

_____

_____

_____

_____

5. Verse 21 cautions fathers not to provoke their children "lest they become discouraged." Why must parents, especially fathers, guide their children with gentleness, and how can this approach impact their spiritual development?

_____

_____

_____

_____

6. In verses 22-23, Paul instructs servants to obey their earthly masters "with sincerity of heart" and to "work heartily, as for the Lord." How does this guidance apply to modern work relationships, and how can believers embody these principles in their jobs today?

_____

_____

_____

_____

STUDY SUMMARY

Colossians 3:17-4:1 instructs believers to live in a way that reflects Christ's character in every word and deed, promoting humility, love, and respect within family and work relationships. Paul emphasizes that, whether leading or serving, all should act with integrity and justice, knowing they are accountable to Christ, the ultimate Master.

ATHLETE CONNECTION

The complete athlete models Christlike character in every interaction, demonstrating humility, respect, and integrity, always mindful of their ultimate accountability to Christ as the true Master.

KEYS TO WINNING

▶ **VIDEO GUIDE AT KINGDOMSPORTS.ONLINE**

▶ LIVE FOR CHRIST IN EVERY WORD AND DEED

Paul calls believers to do everything "in the name of the Lord Jesus," which means that their speech and actions should reflect Christ's character. This message reminds us that all aspects of life—home, work, or public—are opportunities to honor Christ.

1. In what areas of your life do you find it challenging to reflect Christ's character, and how can you intentionally invite Him into these areas to honor Him through your words and actions?

_____

_____

_____

_____

2. How can you make "doing everything in the name of the Lord Jesus" a daily mindset that guides your interactions, decisions, and responsibilities?

_____

_____

_____

_____

▶ PRACTICE HUMILITY, LOVE, AND INTEGRITY IN RELATIONSHIPS

Paul's instructions for family and work relationships emphasize mutual respect, compassion, and just treatment, showing that Christlike love should shape every relationship. Everyone is encouraged to act with integrity and humility, whether leading or following.

1. How can you show greater humility and compassion in your interactions with others, especially those who may be difficult to love or respect?

_____

_____

_____

_____

2. How does acting with integrity impact the trust and respect within your relationships, and what steps can you take to ensure that your actions consistently align with your values?

_____

_____

_____

_____

▶ REMEMBER ACCOUNTABILITY TO CHRIST

For those in positions of authority, Paul's reminder that Christ is the ultimate Master calls for leadership marked by fairness and justice. This takeaway encourages us to lead with a sense of responsibility, knowing we answer to God for how we treat others..

1. How does knowing you are accountable to Christ influence how you lead and make decisions, especially when facing pressures or challenges in your role?

_____

_____

_____

_____

2. In what areas of leadership can you improve your ability to treat others fairly and respectfully, knowing that Christ values and observes each interaction?

_____

_____

_____

_____

GAME CHANGER

This section challenges us to live purposefully, dedicating every word and deed to Christ. Paul calls us to represent Jesus in what we do and how we do it, whether at home, in relationships, or in the workplace. This passage reminds us that every aspect of our lives is an opportunity to honor Christ, making our everyday routines reflect His character. When we approach each task and interaction with this mindset, even ordinary moments become acts of worship that deepen our faith and point others to Jesus.

Paul emphasizes the importance of humility, love, and integrity. He calls us to lead and serve with compassion, treating others with respect and fairness, whether in a position of authority or following someone else's lead. This Christlike approach to relationships fosters an environment of grace, harmony, and mutual support, mirroring God's love in practical ways. By choosing humility and kindness, we create spaces where people feel valued, respected, and loved, embodying the heart of the gospel.

Paul's reminder that Christ is the ultimate Master gives us a perspective that transforms how we view authority and accountability. In all our roles, we ultimately serve Christ, answering to Him for our actions and how we treat others. This sense of accountability inspires us to lead with justice and compassion, aware that our actions have eternal significance. Embracing this call to live in integrity and love, we become witnesses of the gospel, showing that a life rooted in Christ's character can bring light, hope, and transformation to those around us.

ONE BIG THING

What is the most significant lesson for you to take with you from this chapter?

_____

_____

_____

_____

_____

_____

_____

_____

_____

_____

_____

_____

_____

_____

_____

_____

_____

_____

_____

_____

_____

IMPACT PRAYER

Heavenly Father, we desire to honor You in every facet of our lives. Empower us to commit each word we speak and every action we take to glorify Your name. Fill our relationships with humility, love, and integrity, reflecting Your character to those around us. Remind us that we are accountable to You above all, and guide us to lead with compassion and fairness. In Jesus' name, Amen.

★ ★ ★

CHAPTER TWELVE
THE COMPLETE ATHLETE
STRIVES FOR WISDOM

COLOSSIANS 4:2-18

STUDY STARTER

When Louis Zamperini was a young athlete, it seemed like he was on a path to greatness. With his incredible talent and determination, he made it to the Olympics and competed on one of the biggest stages in the world. But his life took a drastic turn when he became a bombardier in World War II. After his plane was shot down over the Pacific, Zamperini survived weeks at sea only to face years of brutal captivity as a prisoner of war. Those experiences left him deeply scarred, physically and emotionally and set him on a path of anger, bitterness, and trauma that defined his life after the war.

Back home, Zamperini struggled to find peace. The horrors he had endured during the war weighed heavily on him, fueling a cycle of anger and addiction. He felt stuck, unable to move forward, and was haunted by nightmares of his past. But everything changed in 1949 when he attended a Billy Graham crusade. He heard the gospel there and decided to surrender his life to Christ. That decision became a turning point, allowing him to let go of the pain and bitterness that had controlled him for so long. He began a journey of healing and spiritual growth that completely transformed his life.

After that, Zamperini's life became all about faith, forgiveness, and service. He chose to forgive his wartime captors, even meeting with some of them to extend grace. He also dedicated himself to helping others by sharing his story of survival and redemption, inspiring people to find hope and transformation in their own struggles. His devotion to spiritual growth wasn't just a one-time thing—it was an ongoing process as he deepened his relationship with God, sought healing, and lived out biblical values every day. Zamperini's story shows that true wisdom and maturity come from facing challenges head-on, surrendering to God, and allowing God's Spirit and Word to guide and reshape you from the inside out.

In Colossians 4:2-18, Paul urges believers to "devote themselves to prayer," being "watchful and thankful" (Colossians 4:2), and to live in a way that honors Christ in every area of life. He emphasizes the importance of making the most of every opportunity, speaking and acting with wisdom, grace, and integrity (Colossians 4:5-6). Paul suggests maturity is about becoming well-rounded in Christ—rooted in prayer, love, purpose, wisdom, and actively serving others.

STUDY PASSAGE

4 *² Continue steadfastly in prayer, being watchful in it with thanksgiving. ³ At the same time, pray also for us, that God may open to us a door for the word, to declare the mystery of Christ, on account of which I am in prison—⁴ that I may make it clear, which is how I ought to speak. ⁵ Walk in wisdom toward outsiders, making the best use of the time. ⁶ Let your speech always be gracious, seasoned with salt, so that you may know how you ought to answer each person. ⁷ Tychicus will tell you all about my activities. He is a beloved brother and faithful minister and fellow servant in the Lord. ⁸ I have sent him to you for this very purpose, that you may know how we are and that he may encourage your hearts, ⁹ and with him Onesimus, our faithful and beloved brother, who is one of you. They will tell you of everything that has taken place here. ¹⁰ Aristarchus my fellow prisoner greets you, and Mark the cousin of Barnabas (concerning whom you have received instructions—if he comes to you, welcome him), ¹¹ and Jesus who is called Justus. These are the only men of the circumcision among my fellow workers for the kingdom of God, and they have been a comfort to me. ¹² Epaphras, who is one of you, a servant of Christ Jesus, greets you, always struggling on your behalf in his prayers, that you may stand mature and fully assured in all the will of God. ¹³ For I bear him witness that he has worked hard for you and for those in Laodicea and in Hierapolis. ¹⁴ Luke the beloved physician greets you, as does Demas. ¹⁵ Give my greetings to the brothers at Laodicea, and to Nympha and the church in her house. ¹⁶ And when this letter has been read among you, have it also read in the church of the Laodiceans; and see that you also read the letter from Laodicea. ¹⁷ And say to Archippus, "See that you fulfill the ministry that you have received in the Lord." ¹⁸ I, Paul, write this greeting with my own hand. Remember my chains. Grace be with you. (ESV)*

STUDY HELP

- *"prayer"*—In Colossians 4:2, Paul exhorts the believers to "continue steadfastly in prayer," emphasizing persistence and dedication in their prayer life. The phrase "being watchful in it with thanksgiving" adds layers to the concept of prayer, combining alertness with gratitude.

- *"best use of time"*—This term carries the idea of purchasing something completely or reclaiming it, specifically in this case, time. Sometimes translated as "redeeming the time," it suggests actively seizing every favorable moment to reflect Christ and advance the gospel. Time is a valuable commodity that can be "bought back" or rescued from being wasted.

- *"seasoned with salt"*—In ancient times, salt was valuable for preserving qualities and enhancing flavor. In Colossians 4:6, Paul uses this metaphor to describe how believers' speech should be engaging, pure, and preserving the truth. These rituals underscored the importance of holiness and cleanliness in approaching God, symbolizing the removal of sin and the restoration of a right relationship with Him.

STUDY QUESTIONS

1. In verse 2, Paul encourages believers to "continue steadfastly in prayer." What does it mean to be persistent and watchful in prayer, and how can you incorporate thanksgiving into your prayer life?

_____

_____

_____

_____

2. Paul asks for prayer that God would "open a door for the word" (verse 3). How does this show Paul's dependence on God for opportunities to share the gospel, and how can you apply this dependence in your own life?

_____

_____

_____

_____

3. In verse 5, Paul calls believers to "walk in wisdom toward outsiders." What does it look like to walk in wisdom, especially when interacting with those who may not share your beliefs?

_____

_____

_____

_____

4. The phrase "redeeming the time" in verse 5 suggests using every opportunity wisely. What does it mean to redeem the time, and how can you ensure that your daily life reflects this principle?

_____

_____

_____

_____

5. In verse 6, Paul encourages believers to let their speech be "gracious, seasoned with salt." How can gracious and thoughtful speech help you represent Christ in your interactions?

_____

_____

_____

_____

6. Verses 7-18 include Paul's final greetings, acknowledging his team members and fellow workers. What do these personal greetings reveal about the importance of community and partnership in ministry?

_____

_____

_____

_____

STUDY SUMMARY

Colossians 4:2-18 encourages believers to be devoted in prayer, wise in their interactions, and intentional in their speech, making the most of every opportunity to represent Christ. Paul's final greetings emphasize the importance of community and partnership in ministry, showing how mutual support strengthens the work of the gospel.

ATHLETE CONNECTION

The complete athlete embraces steadfast prayer, wise interactions, and intentional speech, using every opportunity to reflect Christ's character.

KEYS TO WINNING

▶ **VIDEO GUIDE AT KINGDOMSPORTS.ONLINE**

▶ BE DEVOTED IN PRAYER WITH GRATITUDE

Paul encourages believers to remain steadfast in prayer, watching and giving thanks. This highlights the importance of maintaining a close, thankful relationship with God, relying on Him for guidance and strength.

1. In what areas of your life do you struggle with maintaining steadfast prayer, and how can incorporating gratitude help you deepen your connection with God in those areas?

_____

_____

_____

_____

2. How does regularly giving thanks in prayer shift your perspective on life's challenges and remind you of God's faithfulness?

_____

_____

_____

_____

▶ MAKE THE MOST OF EVERY OPPORTUNITY

Paul calls believers to "walk in wisdom" and "redeem the time," emphasizing intentionality in how we interact with others, especially non-believers. This encourages believers to actively seek ways to share their faith and to be mindful of the impact of their words and actions.

1. How can you become more intentional about using everyday interactions as opportunities to reflect Christ's love, especially with those who may not share your beliefs?

_____

_____

_____

_____

2. In what areas of your life might you be overlooking opportunities to share your faith, and how can you start to redeem the time in those moments?

_____

_____

_____

_____

▶ VALUE COMMUNITY AND PARTNERSHIP

Paul demonstrates the importance of community and mutual support in ministry through his final greetings. His acknowledgment of fellow workers shows that the work of the gospel is strengthened by collaboration, encouragement, and shared purpose among believers.

1. How can you actively support and encourage others within your community, recognizing the importance of partnership in your shared faith journey?

_____

_____

_____

_____

2. In what ways have you experienced growth or encouragement through your relationships with other believers, and how can you intentionally invest in these partnerships?

_____

_____

_____

_____

GAME CHANGER

In Colossians 4:2-18, Paul encourages believers to stay devoted to prayer, with hearts rooted in gratitude. This commitment to constant, thankful prayer shapes our perspective, reminding us to rely on God's guidance and strength in every situation. As we remain watchful and alert in prayer, we develop a closer relationship with God, finding peace in His presence and purpose. Gratitude in prayer keeps our focus on God's faithfulness, helping us see His work even in challenging times and preparing us to face the world with a heart grounded in Him.

Paul also calls believers to "walk in wisdom" and "redeem the time," reminding us to make the most of every opportunity to reflect Christ's character to others. Living with intentionality means recognizing that each interaction is an opportunity to demonstrate Christ's love and truth. Making wise choices and using time well builds a stronger witness for Christ and deepens our understanding of His purpose for us.

Finally, Paul's personal greetings and acknowledgment of fellow workers highlight the power of community and partnership in the gospel. He shows us that ministry is not a solo effort but a collaborative journey where believers support, encourage, and uplift one another. Just as Paul valued his companions, we, too, are called to invest in relationships that strengthen our faith and unite us in God's mission.

ONE BIG THING

What is the most significant lesson for you to take with you from this chapter?

_____
_____
_____
_____
_____
_____
_____
_____
_____
_____
_____
_____
_____

IMPACT PRAYER

Lord, Help us to use every moment and interaction as an opportunity to reflect Your love and wisdom to those around us. Teach us to walk intentionally, make the most of our time, and invest in Your church. May our lives reflect Christ, united in purpose and grounded in Your grace. In Jesus' name, Amen.

NOTES:

_____
_____
_____
_____
_____
_____
_____
_____
_____
_____
_____
_____
_____
_____
_____
_____
_____
_____
_____
_____
_____

CONCLUSION

These are the titles of each chapter you studied. Circle the two that carried the most significance to you in your pursuit of being The Complete Athlete.

Week 1	Colossians 1:1-8	REJOICES in Maturity
Week 2	Colossians 1:9-14	PRAYS for Maturity
Week 3	Colossians 1:15-20	EXALTS Christ
Week 4	Colossians 1:21-33	REMAINS Steadfast
Week 5	Colossians 1:24-29	LABORS for Others to Mature
Week 6	Colossians 2:1-7	PURSUES Mature Knowledge
Week 7	Colossians 2:8-15	GUARDS Against Deception
Week 8	Colossians 2:16-23	REJECTS Self-made Religion
Week 9	Colossians 3:1-11	PUTS OFF the Old Man
Week 10	Colossians 3:12-16	PUTS ON the New Man
Week 11	Colossians 3:17-4:1	SERVES Christ in Everything
Week 12	Colossians 4:2-18	STRIVES FOR WISDOM

Take this opportunity to write out a prayer to God that articulates your desire to be a complete athlete who praises the Lord and leads others to do the same. Especially ask Him to help you grow in the two areas you circled above.

_____

_____

_____

Write down the names and descriptions of the people who participated in this study so that you can remember them and the contribution they made to your spiritual growth.

_____

_____

_____

www.ingramcontent.com/pod-product-compliance
Lightning Source LLC
LaVergne TN
LVHW051244080426
835513LV00016B/1733